The
Boat
Officer's
Handbook

The Boat Officer's Handbook

by Lieutenant David D. Winters, U.S. Navy

Naval Institute Press
Annapolis, Maryland

Copyright © 1981
by the United States Naval Institute
Annapolis, Maryland

Second printing, 1988

Library of Congress Cataloging in Publication Data
Winters, David D., 1953–
    Boat officer's handbook.

    Bibliography: p.
    Includes index.
    1. United States. Navy—Boat officers—Hand-
books, manuals, etc. 2. Boats and boating—
Handbooks, manuals, etc. I. Title.
V880.W56   623.88'123   81–607042
ISBN: 087021–102–1   AACR2

Printed in the United States of America

For
Debbie Elaine Tipton Winters
I told you so.

Contents

Preface

"A ship is known by her boats." This old adage is as true today as it was two hundred years ago, and sharp, efficiently run boats will always win respect and admiration for their parent ships. But running boats is not as simple as it used to be. A properly equipped boat today may require not only the services of a boatswain's mate in order to maintain it, but also those of an electronics technician, an engineman, an electrician, and a hull technician. The administrative complexities that this joint endeavor may raise should be obvious.

The responsibility involved has also increased manyfold, for one liberty boat today may carry enough men to make up an entire sailing man-o-war crew. To assign or accept accountability for the safety of so many lives is not a duty that can be taken lightly. In addition, the military and civil rules and regulations that govern the conduct of vessels large and small have become quite intricate.

In short, the management and operation of ships' boats has become a complex function of considerable responsibility. It is the purpose of this book to aid in preparing officers for the assumption of this responsibility. The reader will find that the material is presented in such a way as to be easily comprehended by the newly initiated ensign, while at the same time it is explained in terms concise enough and in enough depth to serve as a reference and review source for the experienced officer.

It should be a useful source of information and instruction to recently commissioned or about-to-be-commissioned officers, officers of deck divisions, and any other officers at sea or ashore who may, through boating, deck watches, or even unexpected duty as a lifeboat officer, become involved in the management or operation of small craft. But above all, it is intended as an easily carried "take-along" reference for the man who would have the most frequent need for the information contained herein—the boat officer.

The
Boat
Officer's
Handbook

1 Responsibility and Chain of Command in Boats

Authority in Boats

The U. S. Navy Regulations state that, "Except when embarked in a boat authorized by the Chief of Naval Operations to have an officer or petty officer in charge, the senior line officer (including commissioned warrant and warrant officers) eligible for command at sea has authority over all persons embarked therein, and is responsible for the safety and management of the boat."

The reference to warrant officers is further illuminated under the heading "Officers of the Naval Service," where it is stated that "Chief warrant officers and warrant officers whose technical specialty is within the cognizance of a staff corps are classed as chief warrant officers or warrant officers in the staff corps. All other chief warrant officers and warrant officers are classed as in the line." And under the "Succession to Command" headings, it is explained that in ships, chief warrant, warrant, and limited duty officers in the line who are authorized to perform all deck duties afloat may succeed to command.

In addition to unrestricted line officers, therefore, limited duty officers and warrant or chief officers of the line can also be qualified as boat officers and hold ultimate responsibility for a boat's safety and conduct.

Naval custom also dictates that when an insufficient number of commissioned officers or warrant officers are available, chief petty officers of the deck ratings may also be assigned as boat officers, their eligibility for this responsibility being conferred by virtue of their expertise in that area of seamanship.

Chain of Command aboard Boats

The boat officer (when assigned) will be responsible to the officer of the deck for the safe and proper operation of his boat and the proper conduct of personnel embarked. He reports to the officer of the deck or embarked senior line officer eligible for command at sea for his orders and any special instructions that may be applicable. Reporting to the boat officer are the coxswain and the passengers embarked.

The coxswain has, subject to the orders of the OOD and boat officer or senior line officer embarked, full authority over the boat, its crew, and its passengers in all matters concerning safety and operation of the boat. The boat officer will not normally interfere with the coxswain in the performance of his duties, nor will the senior line officer normally overrule, or relieve, either of them. This is a situation that resembles the relationship of a commanding officer on the bridge to his officers of the deck. The authority to relieve is present, but should be exercised only in cases where necessity demands.

The orders of the OOD to the coxswain (or boat officer) will not normally be modified by any passenger. Anyone who does alter them must have due cause and immediately assumes full responsibility for the consequences of his actions.

Duties and Responsibilities

Duties and responsibilities of ship's personnel in regard to boating are delineated in OPNAV 3120.32 articles 453, 456, 630.1 and 720.4. The following is a consolidation of these regulations and guidelines:

The *training officer*, as directed by the commanding officer, shall institute courses of instruction that will serve to indoctrinate all line officers in their responsibilities regarding boat safety and management.

The *executive officer* shall:

- Promulgate boat schedules.
- Designate the proper uniform for boat-crews to conform to local regulations.
- Exercise overall supervision of boating. In the absence of the executive officer, the command duty officer shall perform this function.

The *navigator* shall:

- Provide the officer of the deck and boat coxswains with a section of the appropriate harbor chart showing the ship's berth, other occupied anchorages, all commonly used landings and compass courses thereto, and a copy of local traffic rules and navigational dangers and aids.
- Take action necessary to calibrate or repair boat compasses. Maintain a calibration table in each boat and inspect it frequently for accuracy.
- Provide each boat with a compass course (boat log) book and inspect it daily when boats are in use to ensure that it is properly maintained. (See table 1.)
- When weather conditions dictate, see that a qualified quartermaster or signalman with required signal equipment is a member of the boat crew.
- In conjuction with the first lieutenant, brief all boat officers prior to entry into a port where boats will be required.

The *first lieutenant* shall:

- Qualify personnel as members of boat crews.
- Provide competent crews for all boats permanently or temporarily assigned in accordance with this bill.
- Take timely and positive action to ensure that there are trained boat-crew replacements ready at all times.
- Ensure that all personnel of boat crews are qualified swimmers.
- Conduct thorough training for all personnel assigned to boat crews. This training shall include instruction in : Rules of the Road; boat seamanship; sea manners; boat etiquette and discipline; and safety precautions.

Table 1. Boat Log Sample Form

Destination	Number of Passengers	Departure Time	Arrival Time	Heading	Speed	Comments (If Any)

• Require coxswains to check and record compass courses and running times during boat trips in both fair and foul weather.

• Supervise the daily inspection of the ship's boats and equipment, and cause the report of such inspection to be entered in the ship's log. This shall include proper inspection of the engine, hull, lights, boat gear, and emergency equipment, and a test of the fog signal.

• Be responsible for the operation, care, and maintenance of the ship's boats, except boat machinery.

• Train and certify the qualifications of all boat officers. (An excerpt from *Navy Personnel Qualification Standards* (PQS) concerning Boat Officer Theory may be found in Appendix E.)

• In conjuction with the navigator, brief all boat officers prior to entry into a port where boats will be required.

• Be responsible, under the supervision of the executive officer, for maintaining the boat bill.

The *engineer officer* is responsible for:

• The training and assignment of sufficient qualified boat engineers.

• The operation, care, and maintenance of boat machinery and electrical installations.

• Conducting boat repairs within the capacity of the ship's force.

• Fueling boats prior to 0800 daily.

• Providing personnel to conduct the daily inspection of boat machinery and electrical installations.

The *officer of the deck* shall:

• Exercise direct supervision over operations of ship's boats, and comply with both the boat schedules published by the executive officer and the orders of the commanding officer and other proper authority.

• Ensure that boats are operated in a safe manner and that all boat safety regulations are observed.

• Ensure that boats are not overloaded, and reduce the allowed loading capacity to a safe margin when weather conditions require caution.

- Use boat officers under such conditions as the following: When foul weather or reduced visibility exists or is expected, and on trips of long duration; for first boat trips in foreign or unfamiliar harbors, and at all times when required by local regulations; for large liberty parties returning after sunset, especially prior to sailing.
- Notify the command duty officer when weather or other conditions make the use of a boat officer advisable.
- Require all boat passengers and crew to wear life jackets when weather or sea conditions are hazardous.
- Give particular attention to changes in wind or sea conditions that may affect the safety of boats and embarked personnel, and notify the command duty officer when weather conditions are such that the suspension or resumption of boating is deemed advisable.
- Ensure that harbor charts are provided to boat coxswains, and that boat coxswains understand the navigational information provided by the navigator.
- Ensure that boats are fueled and inspected prior to 0800 daily, that they are clean and smart, that the crew is in proper uniform, and that all boats assigned trips are fully equipped, manned, and fueled and that all equipment is in working order.
- Require one member of the boat crew to act as a bow lookout. This requirement is of major importance to boats such as LCMs, where the coxswain's vision ahead is severely limited.
- Give boat coxswains their trip orders and their orders to shove off.
- Inspect boats secured alongside hourly. If weather or sea conditions render safety doubtful, take immediate action to hoist boats in or send them to a safe haven.
- In port, require the coxswain of the lifeboat to inspect and report to him daily at sunset the condition of the lifeboat as to readiness for service; and at sea require a similar inspection and report at the beginning of each watch.

The *boat officer* (when assigned): will be responsible to the officer of the deck for the safe and proper operation of his boat and the proper conduct of all personnel embarked. Boat officers will be qualified and assigned in accordance with the current directives.

The boat officer (when assigned) shall:

- Man his boat when called away.
- Ensure that the boat coxswain has received and understands his orders.
- Ensure that his boat has a chart covering the route to be followed and that the Rules of the Road and proper boat etiquette are observed at all times.
- Ascertain if he is the senior line officer, eligible for command at sea, embarked in the boat. If he is not the senior line officer embarked, ensure that the senior line officer embarked, eligible for command at sea, is cognizant of this fact.
- In time of danger or emergency, give such orders to the coxswain as he may deem necessary to avoid the danger. If he is not the senior line officer eligible for command at sea, ensure that such embarked senior line officer is made cognizant of the danger or emergency.
- Require life preservers to be worn by the crew and passengers when operating under adverse weather conditions.
- Ensure that the capacity of the boat is not exceeded and that the number of passengers is reduced as sea conditions dictate.
- Be thoroughly familiar with the Rules of the Road in fog. A boat officer will not commence a boat run if the boat, crew, or passengers may be endangered because of reduced visibility.
- Require the boat crew and all personnel embarked in his boat to comply with regulations concerning safety and conduct and be responsible to the commanding officer for the enforcement of boat regulations.

Coxswains are responsible for operating their boats in the following manner:

- Rules of the Road must be obeyed strictly. Especially important to boat coxswains is the Rule of Good Seamanship, which requires that boats give way to ships and seaplanes. Boats should turn away from ships or seaplanes early and radically to show clearly their intentions not to embarrass the larger and less maneuverable vessels.

- Boats must not cut close across the bow or stern of a ship moored or anchored or pass close around the corner of a pier, except when such procedure cannot be avoided. Coxswains must run slowly until there is no danger of collision with any boat that may be obscured.
- Boats must run dead slow when passing other boats that are alongside ships or landings, when in narrow or crowded waters, and when passing deeply laden boats.
- Coxswains must record courses and en route times to all landings visited under various conditions of tide.(See Table 1.)
- Ensure that the boat crew and personnel embarked comply with all safety regulations.
- When a boat officer is not assigned, coxswains will fulfill the duties and responsibilities normally handled by the boat officer.

Required Inspections, Reports, and Instructions

The Boat Bill

Policies and procedures concerning the ship's boats, and definitions of the duties and responsibilities of ship's personnel in regard to boating are set forth in the *boat bill*. Each vessel is required to prepare a boat bill that is tailored to her specific needs. General guidelines and regulations for this bill are set forth in *Opnav Instruction 3120.32*, Article 630.1. At a minimum, the boat bill should contain:

- A consolidation of all pertinent directives and instructions concerning boats and boating.
- The responsibilities and organization of personnel concerned with boating.
- A list of all the ship's boats, their capacities, important characteristics, and required equipment and equipage for each.

- Readiness and inspection checklists.
- The ship's policies concerning boat crew and officer qualifications.
- Special limitations and precautions to be applied in low visibility or inclement weather operations.
- Special procedures and parameters peculiar to your boats or handling gear.
- Procedures to be followed in case of collision, grounding, or other mishap, especially any involving civilian property.
- A copy of the "Standing Orders to Coxswains."
- Anything else considered singularly important.

Daily Boat Report

It is the first lieutenant's responsibility to supervise the daily inspection of the ship's boats and equipment, and cause the report of such inspection to be entered in the ship's log. This shall include proper inspection of the engine, hull, lights, boat gear, and emergency equipment, and a test of the fog signal. A sample boat inspection checklist is contained in Appendix B.

Coxswain's Lifeboat Inspection

The duty lifeboat coxswain is required to conduct an inspection of his lifeboat (rescue boat) at the beginning of each watch underway and at sunset each day when in port, and to report its condition as to readiness for service to the officer of the deck.

Boat Log

Coxswains are required to record courses and en route times (at a given speed) to all landings visited, including tide conditions, during boat trips in both fair and foul weather. This compass-course book is to be inspected daily by the navigator when boats are in use.

Besides this required information, coxswains should also record the number of passengers boarding and disembarking at each stop. This data helps the coxswain avoid overloading his boat, and in the event of catastrophic accident, an accurate record of the number of souls on board can make the implementation of search-and-rescue operations much more efficient and effective—not to mention the amount of unecessary grief and pain it may save. A suggested form for use in the boat log is illustrated in table 1.

Standing Orders to Coxswains

Each boat is required to carry a set of "Standing Orders to Coxswains." The contents might include inspection requirements, safety precautions, operational limits or restrictions, and any other important orders, instructions, or information.

Sovereign Status of Ship's Boats under International Law

In all matters concerning the rights, privileges, and comity of nations, boats that are integral elements of a ship or aircraft are regarded as part of the vessel to which they belong. All persons embarked in a ship's boat, therefore, enjoy the same status and are entitled to the same protection and security as if they were aboard the mother craft.

For this reason, in ports where war, insurrection, or armed conflict exist or threaten, the commanding officer should take special care to require that any boat away from the mother vessel has an appropriate and competent person in charge, and ensure that its nationality is evident at all times. (See U.S. Navy Regulations, Article 0747.)

Refuge and Political Asylum

The subject of granting asylum or refuge is a delicate one with far-reaching repercussions. If, while in charge of a small craft, one is faced with a request for political asylum or refuge and protection, the following instructions and requirements (from Navy Regulations, Article 0940) should be obeyed.

On the high seas, or in territories under exclusive United States jurisdiction:

An applicant for asylum will, at his request, be received on board any naval craft.

Under no circumstances shall the person seeking asylum be surrendered to foreign jurisdiction or control, unless at the personal direction of the Secretary of the Navy or higher authority. Persons seeking political asylum should be afforded every reasonable care and protection permitted by the circumstances.

In territories under foreign jurisdiction (including foreign territorial seas, territories, and possessions):

Temporary refuge shall be granted for humanitarian reasons on board a naval craft only in extreme or exceptional circumstances wherein the life or safety of a person is put in imminent danger, such as pursuit by a mob. When temporary refuge is granted, such protection shall be terminated only when directed by the Secretary of the Navy or higher authority.

Foreign nationals who request assistance in forwarding requests for political asylum in the United States will be advised to apply in person at the nearest American Embassy or Consulate.

Personnel of the Department of the Navy shall neither directly nor indirectly invite persons to seek asylum or temporary refuge.

The Rental and Use of Commercial Boats

The rental of commercial boats for transportation of liberty parties or visitors may, in some instances, be authorized. The proper procedures for acquiring authorization for funding and procurement of commercially operated craft will generally be found in the appropriate fleet supply manual.

When procuring commercial boats for these purposes, commanding officers should ensure the safety of all such vessels, including the adequacy of lifesaving equipment, and should ensure that the maximum capacity of the boats is not exceeded.

2 Seamanship

Boat Safety

Boating operations are, in many ways, inherently hazardous. The following precautions, however, if faithfully observed will contribute a great deal toward reducing the danger factors involved and will help to increase the confidence that the rest of the officers and crew have in the safety and dependability of your small craft and its operators. The most effective safety precaution is a vigorous program of preventive maintenance. Most casualties are attributable to improperly maintained equipment rather than to design deficiencies or personnel failure.

General Safety Rules

• See that all nonoperating personnel are clear of the area prior to any boat-handling operation.

• Ensure that qualified operators are present for every operation.

• Do not turn the electric motor on the winch when a boat is being lowered.

• Keep the number of personnel riding in a boat to the minimum required for launching and stowing operations (except in the case of combat-loaded LCVPs and lifeboats).

• Ensure that personnel riding the boat use lifelines when being raised or lowered with the boat.

• Ensure that lifting hooks are secure before a boat is raised or lowered.

• Be alert for any possible malfunction, and act quickly if it occurs.

• Ascertain that stopper bars are removed from the trackways prior to hoisting a boat by davit.

• When paying out empty falls under power, do not stop the winch motor by means of the brake interlock switch. Use the master switch for this purpose.

• Keep the bilges free of oil.

• Be sure all shafts, cables, engines, and other moving or dangerous equipment are covered.

• The coxswain, or boat officer when assigned, shall be responsible to the commanding officer for the enforcement of boat rules and regulations. Passengers (and crew) should obey any orders given by the coxswain or boat officer.

• Personnel embarking should do so in a quiet, orderly manner, filling the foremost thwarts first and working aft. Sit quietly, and where possible, face aft.

• Passengers should keep all parts of their bodies in the boat and off the gunwales.

• Never allow horseplay or any other behavior that might endanger the boat or those embarked.

• No one should needlessly distract the attention of crew members from their duties.

• No one should sit on life jackets. To do so mats the filler and reduces its buoyancy.

• If a boat swamps or capsizes, passengers should stay with the boat or huddle with the other passengers. No one should strike out alone, because a single large group can be found much more easily than several individual swimmers. Swimmers can use life-jacket straps to secure themselves to one another. All too often, lives have been lost needlessly because overconfident swimmers tried to go for help and drowned before they could be found; in most instances, the majority of those who remained with the boat or in a group were rescued.

• If the weather is becoming rough, boat capacity should be reduced accordingly, usually by half.

• No ship's boat shall be loaded beyond the capacities established by the commanding officer and published in the boat bill without specific permission of the command duty officer, and then only in emergencies.

● No person shall smoke in a ship's boat under any circumstances, except as may be authorized by the commanding officer.

● No person other than those specifically designated by the engineer officer shall operate or attempt to operate a boat engine; test, remove, or charge a boat's battery; tamper in any way with the boat's electrical system; or fuel a ship's boat.

● No person shall be assigned as a member of a boat crew unless he is a qualified swimmer; has demonstrated a practical knowledge of boat seamanship, Rules of the Road, and boat safety regulations; and has been duly qualified for his particular assignment by the first lieutenant.

● All persons in boats being hoisted in or out or hung in the davits shall wear vest-type, inherently buoyant life preservers properly secured. Additionally, under wartime conditions they shall wear battle helmets with the chin straps unfastened and under normal conditions shall wear construction helmets (safety helmets) having a quick breakaway device, with chin straps fastened.

● No boat shall be hoisted aboard ship or lowered with water in the bilges in excess of that which could normally be removed by the installed bilge pumps. In the event that excessive bilge water cannot be removed with the installed pumps, the water should be removed through the hull drain plugs or with a portable pump prior to hoisting aboard or lowering away.

● No person shall board a boat from a boat boom unless another is standing by on deck or in a boat at the same boom.

● All members of a boat's crew shall wear rubber-soled canvas shoes when embarked in a ship's boat.

● All boats leaving the ship shall have local charts with courses to and from their destination recorded thereon and shall have a properly adjusted, lighted compass.

● All boats will have sufficient life preservers on board to accommodate each person embarked, and they shall be readily available when rough seas, reduced visibilty, or other hazards threaten.

• Persons who are intoxicated, sick, injured, or otherwise incapacitated should not be transported by boat without appropriate extra precautions being observed. These precautions should include, at a minimum, the provision of specifically assigned escorts and flotation gear for the incapacitated. Nonswimmers should also be required to wear flotation gear whenever in the boats.

• No boat will be dispatched or permitted to proceed unless released by the OOD. Such release will not be given unless it has been determined that the boat crew and passengers are wearing life preservers, when advisable, and that weather and sea conditions are suitable for small boat operations.

Boat Capacity

Every boat in the naval service is required to be fitted with a label plate that provides data concerning its design, manufacture, and maximum capacity. (See figure 1.) The maximum capacity designated on the label includes the boat crew and

```
BOAT REGISTRY NO. 13681; MAXIMUM CAPACITY,

25 MEN.  {MAXIMUM CAPACITY INCLUDES BOAT

CREW AND PASSENGERS AND ASSUMES ALL PAS-

SENGERS ARE IN COCKPITS AND SEATED SO FAR

AS POSSIBLE.}

NAVAL SHIPYARD, NORFOLK, AUGUST 1939,

BUSHIPS PLAN NO. 248628.
```

Figure 1. Boat manning placard

assumes that all passengers are in the cockpits and are, so far as possible, seated. When carrying liberty parties, the designated carrying capacity should never be exceeded. In carrying stores, the load in pounds, including crew and stores, should never exceed the maximum allowable cargo load, as given on the boat label or as listed in Appendix A. In motor boats, the practice of carrying passengers, stores, or baggage on the top sides should be prohibited. When it is necessary to carry stores or baggage, a corresponding reduction in the maximum number of passengers should be made by decreasing that number by one for every 165 lbs. of cargo taken aboard.

Example: Assume that the coxswain of a 26-foot motor whaleboat (open type) is ordered to make a shore trip to pick up stores weighing approximately 2,000 pounds, and to pick up a liberty party. The rated capacity of a 26-foot motor whaleboat (open type) is 22 men, or in terms of pounds of stores, 22 times 165 or 3,630 pounds. The coxswain should, therefore, pick up the stores (approximately 2,000 pounds) and bring back not more than 8 persons as passengers, for: $(3,630 - 2,000)/165 - 2$ crew $= 8$ passengers.

Reduction in Capacity Due to Weather Conditions

In connection with the rated capacity designated on the label plate, bear in mind that this represents the maximum capacity under normal weather conditions in enclosed waters. Frequently, conditions will be such as to greatly reduce this rated capacity. Reduction is always necessary under extreme weather conditions or in the open sea.

Fatigue

One safety consideration that is often ignored in boating operations is the effect of fatigue on boat crew performance. While hard-and-fast rules cannot be prescribed for the duration of boat crew duty—which may be intermittent in nature—the following general guidelines (table 2) have been recommended by experienced persons for use in assigning LCM crew duty periods, and should be applicable to all medium-sized craft.

It should be recognized that these figures represent the extreme upper limits of a crew's endurance, and except in conditions of emergency, duty periods should be considerably shorter. It also should be understood that an appropriate period of rest (12 to 24 hours) should be provided for the crews between duties of these lengths.

Table 2.   Sea States versus Crew Endurance Hours

Beaufort Scale	Wind	Significant Wave Height	Proposed LCM–6/LCM–8 Crew Endurance
0–2	Light	.3 Ft	16 Hrs
3–4	Moderate	3.5 Ft	10 Hrs
5–6	Strong	6 Ft	7 Hrs
7–8	Gale	10 Ft	3 Hrs

Relative to the scale above, an additional factor should be the temperature. Extremely hot or cold days also decrease crew endurance. Normal peacetime operations are usually conducted within the temperature range 50°–90°F. It is recommended that when the temperature is outside of these limits, the endurance times listed above should be reduced by 10 percent for each 5° F. temperature variance.

Fire Hazards in Powerboats

A fire can be serious anywhere, but it is particularly dangerous in a gasoline- or diesel-powered boat. Although boats are equipped with fire-fighting devices, the best safeguard for those concerned with handling boats is an intelligent appreciation of the fire hazards and knowledge of how to eliminate or reduce them. Following is a discussion of some of the more common fire hazards and how they can be avoided.

Cleaning with gasoline. Because gasoline vapor is highly combustible when mixed with air, the use of gasoline for cleaning the engine or bilges is *strictly prohibited.*

Clothing and oily waste or rags. Keep engine space clear of clothing. Cleaning rags and waste must be stowed in a closed container. After use, they must be burned or otherwise safely disposed of. Clean engines, clean engine spaces, and clean bilges are requisites of a safe boat.

Fuel leaks. The presence of fuel in the bilges or in a free state in a boat is dangerous. The fumes may be ignited easily, resulting in a fire. If fuel from a leak (or fuel spilled while fueling) runs into the bilges, the bilges must be washed down, pumped out, dried, and aired thoroughly.

Bilges and sumps. Bilges and sumps must be kept dry and must be washed out frequently to clear them of fuel and oil. The forward and after engine space bulkheads must be tight in the bilges so that liquid and gas will not pass into adjacent compartments.

Poorly insulated exhaust pipe. Improper insulation of the exhaust pipe where it passes through the hull may set the boat afire. Any defects of this type should be reported immediately to the first lieutenant.

Dirty engine. Grease and oil with which an engine may become encrusted will feed a fire, enabling it to get out of control rapidly. The engine must be cleaned at frequent intervals

Electric wiring. Electric wiring is not permitted in the bilges. The battery box must be located outside of a closed engine compartment and should be provided with suitable drip-proof cover. All bare electric terminals must be wrapped with insulating tape.

Battery charging. Charging batteries produces sufficient hydrogen gas, which, if trapped and ignited, will cause an explosion. Batteries should either be charged on deck or moved to an open space in the boat until the operation is completed. The lead-lined receptacle for batteries should be well ventilated.

Smoking and loose matches. Smoking in any powerboat should be discouraged, and smoking and open lights must never be permitted in gasoline powerboats. Only safety matches are allowed on board naval ships and in naval boats.

Boat Fueling Precautions

Special fueling precautions, as outlined in the *Naval Ships Technical Manual*, must be considered while fueling gasoline powerboats, but the following general procedures are applicable for all powerboats.

- Except in emergencies, boats must not be fueled unless in the water, with engines stopped, and clear of other boats.
- If, in an emergency, it is necessary to fuel a boat in its shipboard stowage, adequate fire-fighting equipment shall be provided at this scene.
- Boats shall not be fueled with passengers aboard.
- Except in emergencies, boats shall not be fueled at night.
- Smoking or naked lights are not permitted in the vicinity while fueling.
- Before starting the engine, inspect compartments and bilges, clean and ventilate as necessary.
- Tank-fueling caps shall always be kept in place when not fueling.
- Fueling instructions must be posted in all powerboats.

Boating Accident Reports

In any case of collision with a ship, another boat, a ladder, a float or landing, heavy debris, or a grounding (no matter how slight), report the fact to the CDO immediately on returning to the ship. Make sure that the coxswain completes a damage report to the first lieutenant. If your boat should be involved in damage (real or suspected) to any private vessel, small craft, (or equipment thereof), or any waterfront structure or property, include the following information in your report to the OOD:

- Time of incident.
- Exact location of incident.
- As complete a description as possible of the property damaged.
- Name and address of owner.
- Estimate of the damage done.
- A detailed description of the circumstances leading up to

the damage, including the action of either boats or persons, if applicable.

• Names and addresses of witnesses. Do not admit to any liability on the part of the government (including yourself, members of the boat crew, or other U.S. boats or crews). Do not make any statements as to the repairs the government will guarantee.

Standard Equipment and Equipage

Boat Standard Equipage

Every U.S. Navy boat in active service is required to have the complete outfit of equipment deemed necessary to enable the boat and her crew to perform their normal day-to-day functions and to weather minor emergencies, such as small fires. Formerly, this outfit was issued with the boat, but now it is necessary to requisition part of it. The "Coordinated Ship's Allowance List" (COSAL) includes all the items each boat on your ship is allowed, the items furnished with each boat, and the items it is necessary to requisition.

A copy of each boat's outfit should be available to the boat coxswain and the division boatswain's mate, because most ships inventory each outfit regularly and on special occasions, as when a boat is leaving the ship for an extended period of time. It is a good idea to enter the list in the front of the boat log.

A typical standard boat equipment list for the MK 2 26-foot motor whaleboat is shown in table 3.

When a boat is turned in, the boat's outfit also must be turned in unless the boat is to be replaced by another of the same type. In that case, the outfit is retained on board. If a boat is to be replaced by one of a different type, the only items that may be retained are those allowed for the new boat.

Equipment in Boats

In addition to the equipage required by the COSAL, the *Standard Operations and Regulations Manual*, Article 630.1.5, requires the following items in every boat:

Table 3. Standard Equipage for the MK 2, 26-Foot Motor Whaleboat

● Anchor—marine fluked 16 lb.	1
● Batteries—dry	2
● Bell—3 lb. with bracket	1
● Bracket/mount	1
● Chain assembly—single leg 10 ft.	1
● Compass—magnetic mounted, with light	1
● Extinguisher, fire, CO^2—15 lb.	1
● Fenders	4
● Grapnel—4-lb. marine boat type	1
● Handle Ex switch—Lantern	1
● Hook, boat—8 ft.	1
● Lantern Sub assembly box	1
● Light—external	1
● Grapnel line—with 24-in. eye 1–2-in. line, 90 ft.	1
● Pail—steel	1
● Ring buoys	1
● Rope, manila—3–4 in., 150 ft.	2
● Bow/stern lines—3 in., 30 ft.	

● Two 18-inch life rings must be carried—one forward and one aft in each boat—secured in such manner that they are easily broken out for use.

● Inherently buoyant life jackets, readily accessible, shall be available in boats for all members of the crew and all passengers. The number of personnel allowed in a boat should never exceed the number of life jackets available.

● Lights prescribed by law must be displayed by all boats under way between sunset and daylight or in reduced visibility.

● All boats must carry fog signaling equipment. This shall include an efficient bell and foghorn or other sound-producing mechanical appliance.

● Fueling instructions must be posted in all powerboats.

● Maximum operating speed must be posted prominently and permanently in all boats.

● Boat compasses must be carried in all boats while on trips away from the ship.

● Portable parts of the hull listed in NAVSHIPS *Technical Manual* and the boat outfits listed in the *Hull Allowance* are to be carried in boats at all times when waterborne.

- Compass course books and harbor charts must be in the boats when waterborne.
- Recall and lifeboat signals must be posted in the boats where they may be easily read by the coxswains. (See Appendix D.) (*Note:* Engine signals may also be posted in the boat. See Appendix D.)
- A set of "Standing Orders to Boat Coxswains" shall be prepared and kept in each boat.

Special Equipment

Equipment required for special situations—such as abandon ship, rescue, and crash kits—is delineated in Appendix C.

In addition to these, another piece of equipment required in certain situations is a boat radio. United States law requires that all vessels 26 feet or more in length and *engaged in towing operations* on United States waters carry a bridge-to-bridge radiotelephone capable of transmitting and receiving on a frequency or frequencies in the 156 to 162 MHz band.

Boat Handling

Hoisting Out

Regardless of when or how a boat is hoisted out, the coxswain is responsible for making the boat ready and for getting the crew into the boat. He must make sure that the engineer checks the fuel and tests the engine. He must check the boat plugs and ensure that the regular boat equipment, in good condition, is in the boat. Also, he must see that the slings, if they are to be used, are rigged and that fenders are in place. When the boat is ready in all respects, and each member of the crew is wearing his life jacket and helmet, the coxswain reports to the boatswain's mate in charge. A handy checklist for launching is contained in Appendix B.

Men on deck rig the sea painter, break out ball fenders and steadying lines, clear the deck area of extraneous gear and if using a crane, test it and rig the safety runner and tripping line. (Figure 2).

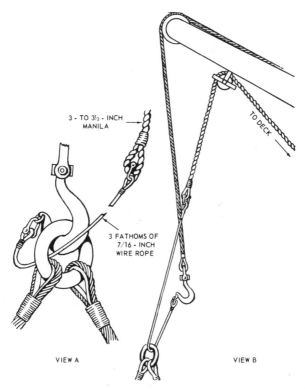

3 - TO 3½ - INCH MANILA

3 FATHOMS OF 7/16 - INCH WIRE ROPE

TO DECK

VIEW A   VIEW B

Figure 2. Safety runner

If the sea is at all rough, there should be at least four steadying lines on the boat, two at each end—one leading well forward, one aft, and the other two inboard. If the position of the boat in its skids allows, the sea painter should be attached to the boat before hoisting.

When ready to hoist away, the whip or falls are set taut, the gripes are released, and men stationed around the boat steady it until it is clear of the skids. The boat is hoisted, then swung over the side and stopped at the rail for the crew to board her.

The sea painter must be adjusted so that when the boat is in the water, the boat tows from the sea painter—not the whip or falls. While the boat is being lowered, two or more ball fenders should be lowered down the ship's side, keeping pace with the boat. Personnel on the steadying lines must prevent the boat from swinging.

Each person in the boat, if not actively engaged in doing something else, must keep a manrope in hand during the lowering and hoisting operations. Manropes are provided for your safety—*use them*. During lowering, it is a good idea to allow the ends of the manropes to hang over the inboard side of the boat. This prevents them from becoming fouled around a leg or other object in the boat and also makes it unnecessary to clear them from the boat once it is waterborne.

In rough weather, the boat's engine should be running while lowering and must always be running before the boat hits the water.

The most dangerous time in hoisting out a boat is the moment it becomes waterborne. For the safety of the crew, as well as the gear, the boat must not be allowed to become waterborne and then snap back on the fall or whip.

Therefore, try to set the boat down when the water under it is comparatively smooth. Judge the roll of the ship and watch the waves. As the ship rolls toward the boat, lower the boat smartly, and release the hook or hooks (aft one first) as soon as it is waterborne.

The boat then rides to the sea painter, and by using the rudder, the coxswain can steer the boat from the ship's side. When the boat gains enough headway to take the strain off the sea painter, the painter is cast off and the end hauled aboard ship by means of the retrieving line.

Hoisting in

In general, the procedure for hoisting in a boat is the reverse of hooking out; but adjustment of the sea painter, so that the boat will tow directly under the falls or whip, is most important.

Once the painter is rigged, it is a good idea to mark it so that thereafter it may be rigged to the correct length, making it unnecessary to readjust it to get the boat in position to hoist.

When ready, the boat comes alongside, the bowhook secures the sea painter, and the speed of the engine is cut back until the boat is towing from the sea painter. By judicious use of the rudder, the coxswain can keep the boat away from the ship's side, yet under the hook(s). Steadying lines should now be passed to the boat.

In the meantime, the person in charge has a chance to watch the rise and fall of the boat, to time it with the roll of the ship, and considering the speed of the hook(s), estimate the best time to hook on. (*Safety note*: Never should anyone be allowed to straddle a leg of a sling during the hooking-on process.)

In heavy weather it normally is best to disembark passengers and crew at the lowest weather deck. Before attempting this, the boat must be snubbed in against the ship's side with frapping and steadying lines.

S.O.R.M. Instructions for Hoisting and Lowering

The *Standard Operations and Regulations Manual* directs that the following precautions be observed while hoisting or lowering boats.

At Night

Normally at night, when anchored in a roadstead overnight, boats that will not be used during the night should normally be hoisted. If hoisting is impractical, adequate steps should be taken to secure them, and they should be frequently inspected. Ship's personnel must be trained in lowering and picking up boats at anchor and under way. Care should be taken not to lower boats in a sea trough or in waters that are too rough for recovery.

Ship's Speed

The ship should not exceed reasonable safe speed when recovering or lowering boats under way. Five knots is the maximum safe speed under calmest conditions. A slight amount of way on the ship will frequently be helpful to the boat crew in hooking the boat to the falls.

Sternway on the Ship

Care must be taken not to pick up or lower boats when the ship has sternway on. If it is necessary to do so, the falls should be hooked or unhooked in reverse of normal order.

Recovering a Boat

When recovering a boat at sea, a course should be selected that gives the ship a minimum roll and provides a lee on the side of the ship where recovery evolutions are in progress. Screws should not be backed in such manner as to throw a wash forward on the recovery side. All hands in the boat should keep a firm grip on the knotted lifelines while being hoisted or lowered. All persons in boats being hoisted in or out by the davits shall wear vest-type inherently buoyant life preservers properly secured. They shall also wear safety helmets.

Overloaded Boats

Boats should not be lowered or hoisted in an overloaded condition. Seven persons in a whale boat, as required for man overboard, are considered maximum load condition for hoisting or lowering. If practicable, personnel other than the regular crew should enter the boat after it is waterborne and should leave it prior to its being hoisted.

Whale Boats as Lifeboats

Whale boats to be used as lifeboats should not be encumbered with rigged canopies. Boats so rigged cannot be lowered or hoisted without danger to the bowhook.

Handling Boats with Davits

There are innumerable designs in davits to accommodate the needs of the ship's boats and ship's structure. This discussion will cover the basic types from which most designs are derived.

Radial Davits

Radial or rounded bar davits rarely are used in the Navy today and are being phased out of service. When the boat is in the stowed position of radial davits, the davit arms point inboard. (See figure 3.) To get the boat out to the lowering position, it must be swung aft until the bow of the boat will clear the forward davit. Next, it must be swung out, forward, and then aft to the lowering position. Before swinging the boat out, it usually is necessary to hoist it high enough for the keel to clear the skids. This may be done by means of a tackle clamped on the hauling part of the falls near the davit head.

Some radial davits are provided with turning-out gears or with levers; both are helpful in swinging the boat around. For davits equipped with levers, however, it is easier and safer to shackle a twofold tackle to each davit head and use the tackles to swing the boat out, one end at a time.

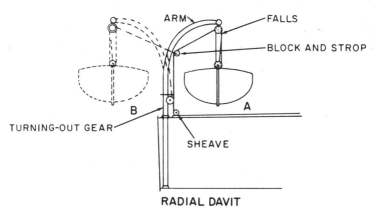

Figure 3. Radial davit

Quadrantal Davits

Quadrantal davits are used chiefly on merchant vessels. The boat rests in chocks under the davits. Outboard sections of the chocks usually are hinged so that, once the weight of the boat is off them, they can be laid flat on the deck, making it unnecessary to raise the boat high enough to clear them in their normal position. Turning a crank that operates a worm gear rises the boat sufficiently high to clear the flattened chocks. Continued cranking racks the boat out to the lowering position. The boat is then lowered away, as with radial davits.

Crescent Davits

The crescent davit and other makes of hinging-out davits (which have largely superseded radial and quadrantal mechanical davits) have been used in all classes of naval vessels, including combatant ships. They generally handle boats of 26 to 30 feet and up to 13,500 pounds. In this type of davit, the arms usually are crescent-shaped and are racked in and out by means of a sheath screw that may be operated by handcrank or by power. (See figure 4.) The boat falls may be of manila or double-braided nylon rope led to the gypsy head of a deck winch, or wire rope led to the drum of a special boat winch furnished with the davits.

Double-Arm Gravity Davits

These gravity davits are most commonly found on newer vessels. There are two primary types; the trackway-pivoted boom or the double-link pivoted type. (See figures 5, 6, and 7.) Gravity davits that handle the larger boats such as LCPLs and LCVPs are generally equipped with a strongback between the davit arms. An electric-powered two-drum winch, located in the immediate vicinity of the davits, provides power to hoist the boats. Cranks can be attached to the winch for hoisting by man power. Power is not required to lower boats. The boat lowers by gravity as it is suspended from the falls, and the descent speed is controlled with the boat davit winch manual brake. Modern gravity

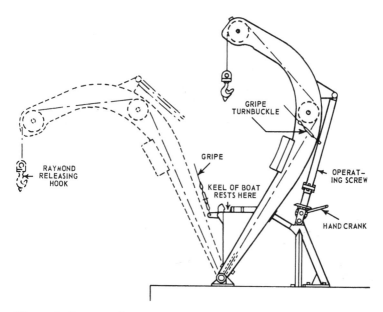

Figure 4. Crescent davits

davits usually have a *falls tensioning device* (such as the one illustrated in figure 8) incorporated into their designs to maintain a constant tension on the boat falls during the final stages of launching or hooking up. Gravity davits are rigged in such a way that when the falls are two-blocked, continued heaving pulls the davit arms up to the stowed position. Keeper bars provided with most trackway davits may then be placed across the tracks and the falls slacked off, allowing the davit arms to rest against the keeper bars. Automatic davit arm latches located at the stowed position are provided with pivoted gravity davits.

At present, either type of gravity davit may or may not be modified. When the falls of the unmodified davit are two-blocked, two pins are inserted through the strongback to hold each movable block in position. The modified davit has movable blocks that latch autmotically when two-blocked.

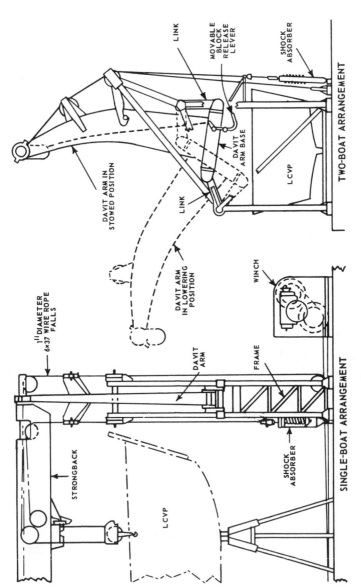

Figure 5. Double-link pivoted gravity davit

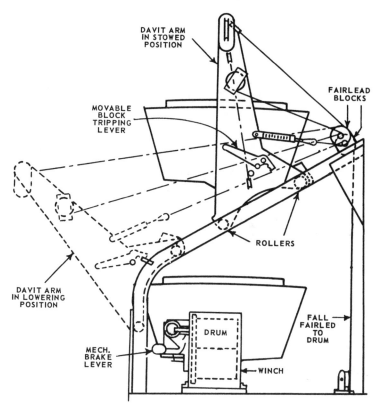

Figure 6. Trackway gravity davit

Depending upon design, a pair of these davits may handle from one to four boats and are designated as single-, double-, triple-, or quadruple-bank davits. In the single-boat arrangement, the boat hangs from the davits or rests in chocks on deck when stowed. The two boats of the double-bank davits are secured in skids, one boat stowed above the other. With the triple- and quadruple-bank davits, one boat is carried at the rail outboard of the two or three other boats, which are nested.

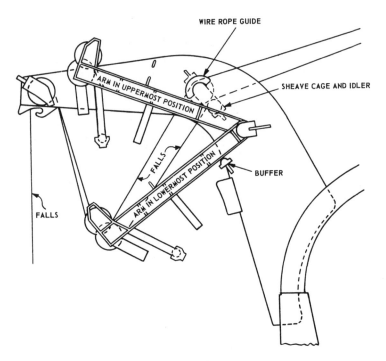

Figure 7. Falls tensioning device

Single-Arm Gravity Davits

The single-arm gravity davit is being introduced on DD-, CGN-, and FFG-class ships. It allows a superior boat-handling procedure and permits the extension of rescue-boat handling to higher sea states than considered safe with conventional double-arm davits. The main features of the single-arm davit that permit this improvement are:

• The use of a single lifting point that minimizes boat hookup time and effort. A newly designed quick-acting hook and special boat bail enable lifting at a single point. Hence, the relatively dangerous and time-consuming process of threading two hooks through bow and stern hoisting rings is eliminated.

• The use of high speed to lift the boat clear of the water as soon as the hook is engaged with the boat bail. Either a hydraulic ram hoist or a two-speed winch (both high and low speed) is provided for lifting the boat at high speed.

A typical trackway, single-arm boat davit arrangement is shown in figure 8. A single-part fall is rove from the single davit head, through a hydraulic ram hoist, to an electromechanically driven single-drum winch. The ram hoist is operated by hydraulic fluid from a nitrogen-charged accumulator and is actuated with a control valve located at the control console.

Beaching and Retracting

For officers of the amphibious fleet, running boats on the beach and retrieving them is a highly developed science that most have ample opportunity to learn, observe, and practice. However, for those of us without boats and equipment specifically designated for this mission, the occasion to beach a boat should be rare. Still, there are times (as during danger or disaster) when it is necessary. If this should become the case, the officer in charge should have a basic understanding of waves and surf and the way to negotiate them. The following instructions concerning this subject are condensed from the *Navy Training Manual for Boatswain's Mate 3 and 2*.

Terms and Definitions (See figure 9.)

Breakers:	A single breaking wave.
Breaker line:	The outer limit of the surf.
Comber:	A wave on the point of breaking. A comber often has a thin line of white water on its crest.
Crest:	The top of a wave, breaker, or swell.
Foam crest:	The top of the foaming water that speeds toward the beach after the wave breaks.
Surf:	A number of breakers.
Swell:	A broad rolling movement of the surface of the water.
Trough:	The valley between waves.

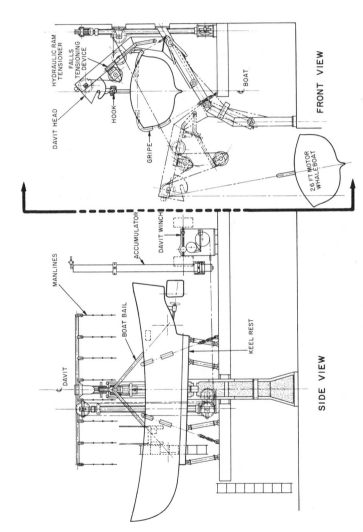

Figure 8. Single-arm trackway gravity davit

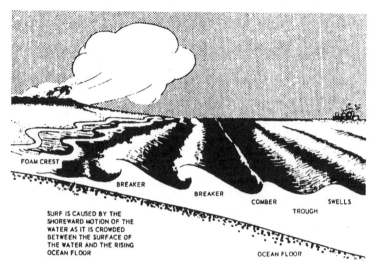

FOAM CREST

BREAKER

BREAKER

COMBER

SWELLS

TROUGH

SURF IS CAUSED BY THE
SHOREWARD MOTION OF THE
WATER AS IT IS CROWDED
BETWEEN THE SURFACE OF
THE WATER AND THE RISING
OCEAN FLOOR

OCEAN FLOOR

Figure 9. Cross-sectional view of surf

Causes and Effects

Surf is caused by the movement of swells toward the beach. As they approach shore, their motion becomes more and more confined due to the decreasing depth of the water. The more shallow the water becomes, the more the crests peak up in the form of combers. This gradual change continues until the rising bottom interferes so much with the stability of the waves that they topple forward as breakers.

Sometimes, two more or less well-defined surf belts are caused by a sand-bar or reef between the outer surf (or breaker line) and the beach.

Breakers vary in size and sometimes may follow a sequence for a short interval—a large breaker following a certain number of smaller ones. There is no regularity to the pattern, so don't, for example, count on every seventh breaker being larger than the six preceding it. The sea just doesn't work that way. The interval between breakers is fairly constant, however, tending to stay the same for several hours. Swells causing surf are created by winds far out to sea, and the interval between swells is determined by the distance the swells travel from their origin, which may be several hundred miles.

The important things to remember about surf are that (1) you must not be lulled into expecting the surf to be constant, (2) you must respect it, and (3) you must make it work *for* you while beaching and retracting.

Beaching

The greatest danger in beaching a boat is that it may broach. Broaching is caused by the surf hitting the boat on a side or quarter, resulting in the boat being thrown broadside onto the beach. The is a dangerous situation, for the boat takes a severe pounding from the waves and may fill with water or even capsize. A boat also can broach in a surf when nowhere near the beach. Usually this is caused by the stern's being raised higher than the bow. The bow is driven into a relatively slow-moving mass of water while the stern comes hurtling on. The inevitable result is that the boat goes stern over bow, casting all hands into the sea. By obeying the following instructions, one should be able to beach a boat in moderate surf without broaching

Before beaching, lie to outside the breaker line and study the situation. Select your landing spot with care, examining the shoreline and the reefs and rocks off shore. They may provide a clue to the location of a lee where you can land without danger. Such a study may also forestall your being surprised by a barely noticeable sandbar or reef that would make it necessary to change course on your way to the beach.

Prior to entering the surf zone, line up your boat with the spot where you intend to beach. You should not change your course inside the breaker line. Estimate the rate at which waves are rolling in, and adjust your speed to ride in just behind the crest of a breaker or comber. Keep your boat perpendicular to the surf. The surf normally goes in parallel to the beach, but the angle of the boat relative to the surf—not to the beach—is the important consideration

If you should ground before arriving at the beach, do not assume that the water is shallow the rest of the way in. Chances are that your boat is on a sandbar, and the water between it and the beach may be several feet deep. Keep your screw turning ahead slowly until a wave lifts the boat, then gun your engine, wait for the boat to be lifted again, and once more speed your engine. Repeat that procedure until your boat is over the sandbar and then proceed to the beach.

Hit the beach at a good speed so that the entire keel grounds. Keep the engine turning over fast enough to hold the boat securely on the beach. Idle down when the water recedes to avoid letting the screw race wildly in shallow water.

Antibroaching lines may help prevent a boat from broaching. The use of these lines on an LCVP is illustrated in figure 10.

Should the engine fail before beaching, wait until the boat is well within the length of your anchor line from the beach; then drop the anchor, pay out the line, and let the boat surge to the beach with each breaker.

To prevent your boat from broaching after hitting the beach (in addition to using antibroaching lines), keep breaking seas dead astern, drive well up on the beach, and gun your engine when waves lift the boat. Line up your bow with some object on the beach so that you will be easily able to tell if the angle of the boat changes.

Sometimes it is possible to free a broached boat without outside help. Put the rudder toward the beach, and when a wave lifts the boat, gun the engine. The resulting discharge current tends to force the stern away from the shore.

If the surf is especially high and your boat is properly prepared, the use of a *sea anchor (drogue)* or a *surfline* may prove advantageous. A sea anchor or drogue is a cone-shaped device often made of cloth or canvas, open at one or both ends (see figure 11.) It is equipped with a towline secured at the large end and a tripping line at the small end. The tripping line is

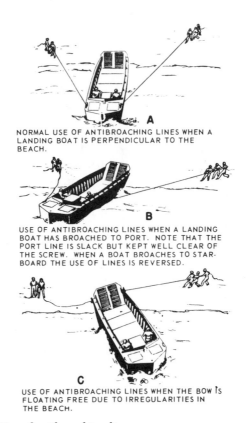

NORMAL USE OF ANTIBROACHING LINES WHEN A LANDING BOAT IS PERPENDICULAR TO THE BEACH.

USE OF ANTIBROACHING LINES WHEN A LANDING BOAT HAS BROACHED TO PORT. NOTE THAT THE PORT LINE IS SLACK BUT KEPT WELL CLEAR OF THE SCREW. WHEN A BOAT BROACHES TO STARBOARD THE USE OF LINES IS REVERSED.

USE OF ANTIBROACHING LINES WHEN THE BOW IS FLOATING FREE DUE TO IRREGULARITIES IN THE BEACH.

Figure 10. Use of antibroaching lines

attached in such a way that by taking in on it and slacking off the towline, the sea anchor can be caused to invert and lose its drag.

A sea anchor towed 40 to 60 yards behind a boat under either power or oars serves to keep the stern, or bow, as appropriate, into the surf. When a large breaker approaches, the tripping line is slacked off and the sea anchor fills and drags. After the breaker passes, the tripping line is secured and the towline is slacked off. In this way the drogue does not impede desired

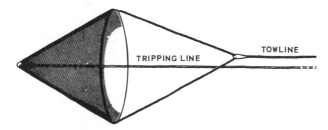

Figure 11. Sea anchor or drogue

progress toward the beach, but definitely assists in preventing the boat from broaching.

If the zone is not too wide, it is sometimes possible to drop anchor outside the breaker line and pay out a *surfline* (200–300 yards) around the samson post or towing bit over the bow or stern. By snubbing the line at the approach of large breakers, and slacking it off after they pass, you can ease a boat to the beach often without using any power. This method is probably the most dependable of all; not only does this method avoid reliance on your engines; it also automatically keeps your boat at the proper angle relative to the surf. In addition, by keeping a slight strain on the surfline after being beached, you prevent the boat from going too solidly aground. This precaution provides for much easier retraction later. Retraction is, of course, accomplished by pulling the boat away from the beach by means of the surfline. The engine, if available, could be used to further facilitate the retraction.

Retracting

It is while being retracted that a boat is most likely to broach. The proper method of withdrawing from the beach is to shift the engine into reverse, wait for a wave to float the boat, and then gun the engine, backing straight out. When the wave recedes, slow the engine and repeat the process with the next until you are floated free. Then continue to back until you are outside the breakers. It is important that during the entire process you do not allow the boat to swing to one side or the other. This is most easily accomplished by sighting over the bow to an object on shore and keeping the two lined up.

Once clear of the surf zone, on the crest of a wave, throw the rudder hard over, shift into forward and gun the engine, and the boat should pivot quickly around and meet the next wave head on.

Towing

Towing is an art in itself. It is more than simply attaching a line to a floating object and going ahead on engines. A ship's boat is frequently called upon to tow disabled boats and small barges, or floats, etc., so a good prior knowledge of the basics of towing is indispensable.

Towing Astern

Motor launches and motor whaleboats are fitted with two single towing bitts, one on either side. When towing astern, a bridle must be made secure to both bitts so as to allow access to the rudder. When the tow line is secured, go ahead slowly on engine until all slack is out of the tow line. Keep an axe or sharp knife ready in case it becomes necessary to cast off immediately. If towing a number of boats in tandem, station a man in the rear boat at her rudder or with a steering oar rigged to steer the last boat, otherwise the entire tow will have a tendency to "whip."

With a long tow, give all buoys and stationary objects a wide berth, for either current or wind, or both, may cause your tow to drift into them.

Towing Alongside

Secure your boat on the tow's quarter (port quarter is best with a right-handed screw), so as to get the benefit of your rudder for steering. Keep men standing by your lines to cast off in a hurry if need be.

To assist a rudderless boat, it is better for the boat in distress to take you in tow and you act as his rudder, depending, of course, on the size of each boat. In this case a bridle is necessary so that you may swing his stern either way by using your rudder and engine, if necessary.

Rescue Boats

Regulations require that a ship at sea have at least one boat rigged and ready for lowering (see Appendix B) to be used as a rescue boat (usually, albeit confusingly, called a lifeboat). A list of required equipment for this boat is contained in Appendix C. Local commands may, of course, add to these requirements as conditions dictate.

At the start of each watch under way, the lifeboat coxswain musters the crew, checks the boat and gear, has the engine tested, and reports to the officer of the deck. In port, this inspection and report are conducted at sunset.

Whenever a situation arises that might require rescue by boat, the boat crew and lowering detail should station themselves immediately at the sounding of the first alarm and simultaneously with shipboard recovery stations. A preappointed officer (usually the JOOD) will be dispatched as the boat officer. The first lieutenant will control the lowering of the lifeboat in accordance with the orders of the commanding officer, and the boatswain's mate of the watch will usually take charge of the lowering detail.

The lowering detail may consist of varying numbers of men and duties depending on ship type. The manning of the rescue boat, however, is delineated by naval regulation (OPNAVINST 3120.32a) as set forth in table 4. Responsiblities of other personnel involved are charted in table 5.

Once a rescue boat is in the water, communication should be established and maintained, preferably by radio, but if needed, back-up systems of lights, flags, semaphore, and/or flares should be available for immediate use. The signals in Appendix D have been specified for use in rescue operations, and the crewmen in charge of communications should be familiar with them. It is, of course, also wise to have a laminated

Table 4. Lifesaving Crew

No. of Personnel	Rate	Duty	Division
1[1]	JOOD	Boat officer with binoculars	na
1[1]	BM 3/2	Coxswain	Deck
1[2]	MMFN	Engineer	Eng
1[1,3]	SM 3/2	Communications/rifleman	OS
1[2]	SA/SN	Bowhook/rifleman	Deck
1[1,4]	HM	Corpsman	H

[1] Must be second class swimmers.
[2] Must be first class and SAR qualified swimmer.
[3] Must be qualified on M1/M14 rifle for shark watch.
[4] Only when two or more are on board ship.
Note: The maximum number of personnel authorized during hoisting/lowering is seven.

copy of these signals included with the boat's regular equipment.

The approach to a survivor should be made in such a way as to keep him on the boat's port bow so that the cast of the screw, when reversed, will set the boat down alongside him. The survivor of an aviation accident, who may still be wearing parachute shroud lines that may be submerged and not visible to the boat crew, should be approached with caution. Wash from the boat screw could catch the parachutes canopy and pull him under, or the screw could get tangled in it.

A streamed parachute should first be hooked and pulled into the rescue boat. This will provide a positive means of preventing loss of the survivor. It has been found that when shroud lines are in the water, the problem of disentanglement increases; therefore, shroud lines should be lifted clear and pulled away from the survivor.

Usually, a swimmer should be put in the water to help bring the victim aboard. All recoveries of a person in the water should be attempted with the person facing the gunwale of the boat to prevent occurrence or aggravation of back injury.

Instructions for conducting rescue operations in conjunction with a helicopter are subject to frequent revision and may be

Table 5. Rescue Responsibilities

Station	Personnel Assignment	Watch Duration	Div	Duties
Fantail life-buoy watch	SA/SN	Continuous 4-hour watch	Deck	Throw life buoy in vicinity of man in water. Spread alarm if necessary.
Lifeboat crews	BM[1], SN[1,2]	Continuous 4-hour watch	Deck	Man boat to recover man.
	FN[1,2]	On call	A div	Ready boat for lowering.
	HM[3,4]	On call	H	First Aid.
	SM[4]	On call	OS	Communications.
Boat-lowering detail	Div	On call	Deck	Lower boat when ordered. Stand by to pick up boat.
Deck rescue detail	2 SA	On call	Deck	Man heaving lines with kapok monkey fists.
	BM, 2 SN	On call	Deck	Lower ladders and nets.
	2 SN[1]	On call	Deck	Stand by in harness to assist man in water.
Special lookouts	4 SA/SN	On call	Deck	Attend lines on swimmers.
Shark watch	2 QM	On call	OS	Keep man in sight.
	GM	On call	Deck	Use rifle fire to drive off a shark only as a last resort and when directed. Use shark repellent where possible.

[1] Must be first-class and SAR qualified swimmer.
[2] In-boat shark watch.
[3] In-boat victim lookout.
[4] Lifeboat crew without active responsibilities at various times.

found in *Shipboard Helicopter Operating Procedures,* Navy Warfare Publication 42.

Weather Phenomena

To those who handle and manage small craft, the weather should hold an especially great significance, for many conditions that larger vessels might take in stride could prove quite dangerous to their smaller kindred, the ship's boats. This chapter deals with some of the more common meteorological phenomena, their causes, and the interpretation of them with a view to foreseeing the weather to come.

Barometric Pressure

Barometric pressure is a compressing force in the atmosphere caused by the weight of the air above. It is, on the average, equal to approximately 14.7 pounds per square inch at sea level. However, it is usually measured in terms of height of a mercury column it could support rather than in terms of psi. Figures 12 and 13 illustrate this and show a conversion table for the two most common scales used.

Temperature

Atmospheric temperature is usually measured in degrees Fahrenheit or degrees Celcius (formerly known as Centigrade). Figure 14 compares the two scales.

Relative Humidity and Dewpoint

Humidity is defined as the amount of moisture (water vapor) contained in a given volume of air. The relationship between the amount of water the air can contain at a given temperature and the amount it actually *does* contain is expressed as a percentage. This percentage is the *relative humidity.* The quantity of water vapor the area can contain varies with the temperature of the air. The cooler a parcel of air is, the less water it can hold. When it cools to the point that it can hold no more water vapor (making its relative humidity 100 percent), it has reached its

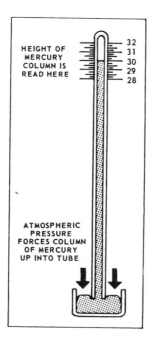

HEIGHT OF
MERCURY
COLUMN IS
READ HERE

32
31
30
29
28

ATMOSPHERIC
PRESSURE
FORCES COLUMN
OF MERCURY
UP INTO TUBE

Figure 12. Atmospheric pressure and mercury barometer

dewpoint, and any more cooling will cause the water to con-
dense—forming clouds, fog, or dew.

Winds

Wind is described in terms of the direction from which it comes
and its velocity. The following tables (tables 6 and 7) will aid
in estimating wind speed, should more sophisticated methods
be unavailable. Direction can be deduced from blowing smoke,
flags, or spray, or from the ripples and wavelets that may run
across the surface of the water as a result of the wind.

Fronts

A front is a line along which air masses of sharply contrasting
properties come in contact. If the colder of the two masses is
dominant, under-riding the warmer mass ahead of it, we have

Table 6. Wind Speed Indicators

Speed (knots)	Indication
Less than 1	Calm; smoke rises vertically.
1–3	Smoke drifts from funnel.
4–6	Wind felt on face.
7–10	Wind extends light flag.
11–16	Wind raises dust, cinders, loose paper, and the like.
17–21	Wind waves and snaps flags briskly.
22–27	Whistling in rigging.
28–33	Inconvenience felt walking against wind.
34–40	Generally impedes progress.

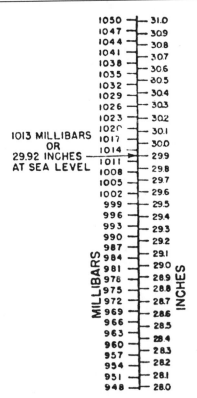

Figure 13. Atmospheric pressure, inches vs. millibars

a *cold front*. If the opposite is true, it is considered to be a *warm front*. And if a cold front (which is always the faster of the two) catches up with and contacts a warm front, an *occluded front* is formed.

Fog

Fog, which is actually a cloud lying on or very near the earth's surface, is a phenomenon that can appear quite suddenly, disorienting boat crews and hiding hazards to navigation. It can be caused by a number of meteorological combinations and is a condition for which the wise boat officer or coxswain is always

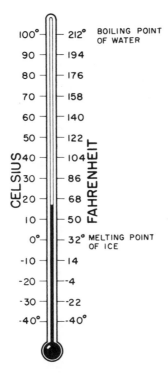

Figure 14. Celcius vs. Fahrenheit

Table 7. Beaufort Wind Scale

Beaufort Number	Knots	Descriptive Terms	Sea criterion 1939 (provisional)	Approx. equivalent sea disturbance scale in open sea		
				Code Fig.	Description	Mean ht. of waves in feet
0	Less than 1	Calm	Sea like a mirror.	0	Calm (glassy)	
1	1–3	Light air	Ripples with the appearance of scales are formed, but without foam crests.	1	Calm (rippled)	½
2	4–6	Light breeze	Small wavelets, still short but more pronounced. Crests have a glassy appearance and do not break.	1		1
3	7–10	Gentle breeze	Large wavelets. Crests begin to break. Foam of glassy appearance. Perhaps scattered whitecaps.	2	Smooth (wavelets)	2½
4	11–16	Moderate breeze	Small waves, becoming longer; fairly frequent whitecaps.	3	Slight	5
5	17–21	Fresh breeze	Moderate waves, taking a more pronounced long form; many whitecaps are formed (chance of some spray).	4	Moderate	9
6	22–27	Strong breeze	Large waves begin to form; the white foam crests are more extensive everywhere (probably some spray).	5	Rough	14
7	28–33	Moderate gale	Sea heaps up, and white foam from breaking waves begins to be blown in streaks along the direction of the wind. (Spray begins to be seen).	6	Very rough	19

8	34–40	Fresh gale	7	Moderately high waves of greater length; edges of crests break into spray. The foam is blown in well-marked streaks along the direction of the wind.	High	25
9	41–47	Strong gale	7	High waves. Dense streaks of foam along the direction of the wind. Sea begins to roll. Spray may affect visibility.		31
10	48–55	Whole gale	8	Very high waves with long overhanging crests. The resulting foam in great patches is blown in dense white streaks along the direction of the wind. On the whole, the surface of the sea takes a white appearance. The rolling of the sea becomes heavy and shocklike. Visibility is affected.	Very high	37
11	56–63	Storm	9	Exceptionally high waves. (Small- and medium-sized ships might be lost to view behind the waves for a long time.) The sea is completely covered with long white patches of foam lying along the direction of the wind. Everywhere the edges of the wave crests are blown in froth. Visibility affected.	Phenomenal	45 or more
12	Above 64	Hurricane/typhoon	9	The air is filled with foam and spray. Sea completely white with driving spray; visibility very seriously affected.		

prepared. Fog is most likely to form when the dewpoint and the actual temperature are very close to each other (within five degrees), or when conditions may cause the air in a certain location to be cooled rapidly, as when a warm, moist wind is blowing across a cold ocean surface; special caution should, of course, be exercised at such times.

Clouds

Clouds are made up of tiny water droplets, which due to various atmospheric phenomena, have condensed from the air "en masse" and have remained suspended in the atmosphere. They are valuable indicators of weather to come for hours or even days in advance. The smart seaman keeps an eye on them.

There are ten basic cloud types, divided into three families according to altitude (high, middle, or low). These are illustrated in figure 15.

High Clouds

Cirrus (Ci). Often called "mares' tails," these clouds appear as delicate plumes or tufts of a fibrous nature and usually are pure white, except at sunrise and sunset. Cirrus are usually considered fair-weather clouds, but if they are followed by lower, thicker clouds, rain or snow should be considered likely within two days or so.

Cirrostratus (Cs). Cirrostratus clouds usually occur as a thin, almost transparent veil. The sun and moon can generally be seen through them in sharp detail, but often will appear to have halos around them. This thin cloud cover, if followed by a heavier, lower cloud cover, is considered an indicator of unsettled or violent weather to come.

Cirrocumulus (Cc). These clouds are also known as "mackerel sky" because of their resemblance to fish scales. Although they usually appear as small white flakes or scales, they may also take on the appearance of small globular shapes. Like cirrus, these clouds are usually considered fair-weather clouds, but if

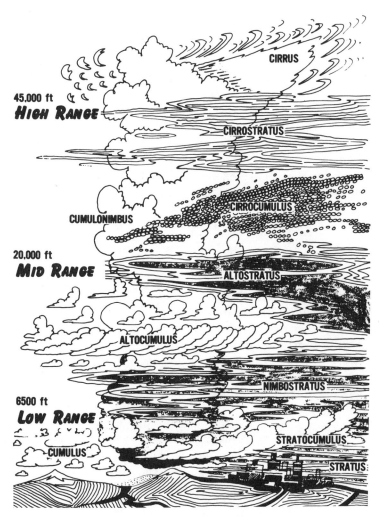

Figure 15. Layer diagram of three families of clouds

they begin to turn gray or thicken, they may foretell the coming of stormy conditions.

Middle Clouds

Altostratus (As). These clouds have the appearance of a gray, translucent sheet of ground glass. The sun and moon shining through them will appear to have solid coronas around them in contrast to the halos produced by cirrostratus clouds. Low, thick altostratus clouds, especially when accompanied by gray, ragged clouds just below them, are harbingers of long-lasting unstable weather with rain or snow.

Altocumulus (Ac). Altocumulus clouds are often shaped like balls or patches joined together at the edges. Occasionally, they will become aligned in long rolls, resembling slowly moving ocean swells. When they thicken and lower, a short but stormy period of showers may be expected.

Low Clouds

Stratocumulus (Sc). Stratocumulus clouds are gray, soft-looking clouds that form in rolls, which move much as do ocean swells—though much more slowly, of course. They are usually followed by clearing skies.

Stratus (St). Stratus clouds form low thick layers that often have few, if any, breaks or inconsistencies, giving the sky the appearance of a flawless gray dome. Strong winds, however, can break up this uniformity, separating the layer into fragments called *fractostratus* clouds. When stratus clouds produce any precipitation at all, it is seldom more than a drizzle.

Nimbostratus (Ns). This is a very low, vaguely defined, dark gray cloud layer, often appearing to have a ragged base. It usually brings mild but persistent precipitation.

Cumulus (Cu). Often called "fair-weather" cumulus, these clouds only appear in patches. Occasionally, flat bases will be apparent on them, but usually they maintain a rugged, cotton-tuft appearance. In spite of their good-weather reputation, when they start to grow vertically, they can speedily turn into cumulonimbus storm clouds.

Cumulonibus (Cb). The cumulonimbus is a huge, towering cloud that is often wider at the top than at the bottom. It always is formed with a horizontal base, but when precipitation begins, this base may be obscured. This type of cloud is also known as a "thundercloud" or "thunderhead" because of the violent lightning and thunder often accompanying the high winds, rain or snow, and hail it brings. Due to the great range of altitude that this cloud may cover from base to top, it is often considered not to be a true member of the high, low, or middle cloud families, but to belong in a separate class of its own.

Rules of Thumb

● In middle latitudes, a barometric pressure of 30.50 inches is considered high and 29.50 is considered low.

● A persistent decrease in pressure predicts foul weather.

● A sudden fall in barometric pressure (over .04 inches per hour) indicates the coming of heavy winds.

● A steady barometric pressure promises fair weather.

● A slowly but consistently rising barometer, especially when coupled with rising temperatures, indicates that the weather is beginning to stabilize.

● A rapid rise in barometric pressure foretells unsettled weather.

● The violence and speed of an approaching storm are indicated by the rate and amount of fall of the barometer. When local weather conditions remain unchanged and barometric pressure drops, a distant storm is raging. If the average fall per hour is .02 inches to .06 inches, the distance from the center of the storm is roughly 150 to 250 miles. If the fall is .06 to .08 inches or .12 to .15 inches, the nearness is about 150 or 100 miles, respectively.

● When cirrocumulus clouds follow altocumulus, expect a thunderstorm.

● A halo around the sun or moon indicates the coming of rainy weather or worse, probably within 24 to 48 hours.

● Swells formed by a storm move out ahead of it and may foretell its coming. These swells are called *storm surge*.

● Warm fronts usually bring gradually thickening clouds, which come closer and closer to the ground, and brief showers that give way to steady rain. As the front passes, the temperature rises and the steady rain stops. The wind shifts (from southeast to southwest in the Northern Hemisphere and from northeast to northwest if south of the equator), and drizzle and fog will probably follow for a time. Warm fronts tend to bring deep, long-lasting fog.

Cold fronts will usually be accompanied by sudden, brief but often violent, thunderstorms, with unpredictable shifting winds called *squalls*. As the front passes, the barometric pressure will rise, the temperature will drop, and skies should clear, all quite quickly. Its passage will also be marked by an abrupt but lasting wind shift away from south or southwest to north or northwest in the Northern Hemisphere. In the Southern Hemisphere the shift would be from north to northwest to south or southwest.

An occluded front tends to produce confused, unpredictable winds and weather.

Regardless of the type of front, its passage will be marked by a dip in the barometric pressure, for every front is, in itself, a low-pressure area.

Buys Ballot's Law

When facing the wind (in the Northern Hemisphere), the center of the low-pressure system lies to the right of and behind you. In the Southern Hemisphere, it is to the left of and behind you.

Maxims

Red sky at morning, sailors take warning. A prolonged red sunrise indicates foul weather later that day.

Red sky at night, sailors delight. A bright red sunset indicates fair weather probable. (See Matt. 16: 2–3.)

In the morning, mountains, in the evening fountains. Large cumulus formations with the rising sun foretell the arrival of storms later that day.

Mares' tails and mackerel scales make tall ships carry low sails. Cirrus and cirrocumulus clouds often precede the arrival of a warm front and its accompanying unsettled weather.

Storm Warnings

Whenever winds dangerous to navigation are forecast for an area, Navy, Coast Guard, and National Weather Service stations, plus many yacht clubs, hoist, in some conspicuous place, flags by day and lights by night to warn all seamen of the expected conditions. Figure 16 lists and explains these signals.

Lifeboat Navigation and Survival

In a survival at sea situation more than in any other involving small craft, preparation is everything. When you find yourself in a 25-man life raft responsible to and for the other 24 lives, it is too late to begin putting together a survival packet or to start studying navigation. The information in this chapter will not prepare you for such a situation, but it will give you a good idea of *how* to prepare yourself.

Leadership and Command

In a lifeboat, as in any other boat, responsibility and command rest with the senior command-at-sea eligible officer aboard. (See chapter I.) It is important that a person-in-charge be established promptly and that his authority be accepted and supported by the rest of the group.

The maintenance and, if necessary, enforcement of order and discipline is imperative for the common good. But this is not to imply that an authoritarian attitude is desirable. Decisions, where practicable, should be made democratically, with the company being informed of the alternatives, the pros and cons of each, and in the best judgment of the officer in charge, the preferred course of action. But never forget that the responsi-

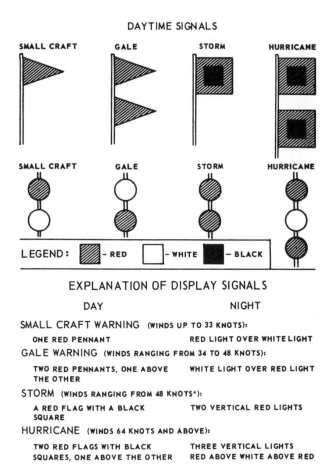

Figure 16. Wind warning signals

bility, and therefore the final word, rests with the officer in charge. A leadership posture such as this will go a long way in promoting the confidence and trust of one's men when rations are getting low and hope is beginning to wane. But before the need arises to address such an abstract issue as leadership methods, there will be more tangible and immediate problems at hand. The following paragraphs deal with these in order of importance.

First Things First

Spend as little time in the water as possible. Better yet, climb aboard your survival craft without entering the water at all. In cold climates, a swimmer's period of useful consciousness may be measured in seconds, and even in a warm environment, prolonged swimming can increase injury from exposure and cause the expenditure of energy that may be vitally needed later on.

If the rafts are overcrowded, however, and the water is not too cold, you may have to let some of the most able-bodied men remain in the water and hang onto the sides of the raft. (Ropes should be provided for this purpose.) But this should only be done when there is no other choice, and then no longer than absolutely necessary.

If using rubber rafts, do not waste precious minutes inflating them one at a time. Activate them all, and then, if you are entering from the water, save yourself and your men some energy by beginning the boarding process while they are still inflating. Boarding a fully inflated raft is more difficult than it looks, and may be nearly impossible for a person who is tired or injured, so if a couple of men are already inside to help the others aboard, everyone will come out ahead.

One note of caution, though. Automatically inflated rafts carry large, heavy bottles of pressurized gas that may, during the first few seconds of inflation, swing around with enough force to injure seriously anyone who happens to get in the way. Therefore, after the raft is initially activated, give it a few seconds to settle down before approaching it.

Sea anchor. If the water is rough, throw out a sea anchor. This will do a great deal to help keep your craft right side up and stable. Sea anchors and their use are explained earlier in this chapter. If one is not provided and you haven't the necessary time or material to make one, even 100 yards or so of bare line tossed overboard with one end attached to your stern will create a surprising amount of drag, and considerably reduce the danger of broaching or capsizing.

Administer first aid to the injured. A later section of this book contains a brief list of "Dos and Don'ts" for emergency non-professional medical care.

Search for survivors. Do not enter the water to recover other victims unless there is no other way to do it. Rather than swimming or paddling over, throw a line.

Salvage all you can. Cups, bottles, canned foods, clothing, even pencils and pens, anything that might be of use should be picked up and stowed securely.

Send out a distress signal. (See Appendix D.) If you have an emergency transmitter, make sure that it is properly used. If it is battery operated, do not allow the power to be exhausted by making radio transmissions unless there is a reasonable chance of someone detecting them. On the other hand, if it is manually driven (as with a crank) allow no lapse in its operation.

Rig protective shelter. Set up canopies or sunshades immediately. If the weather is hot, you will need the shade they provide to help prevent dehydration and sunburn. (The sides can usually be left open for ventilation.) And if it is cold, you will need the protection from wind and spray.

Then, Once Things Have Settled a Bit . . .

You can begin organizing with an eye to the long haul. Stay calm and optimistic, and encourage others to do likewise. Panic or hopelessness, if they gain a foothold, can spread quickly. It helps if everyone is kept busy by work or conversation. A routine is important. Lookout watches, fishing, navigational duties, and other such activities can help fulfill this need. Set up a watch schedule and be sure every lookout knows how to use the signal gear. See that those on watch are alert to prevent pilfering.

Besides immediate first aid, which must be rendered to the seriously injured, there are a number of actions that should be taken to make yourselves more comfortable and prevent further deteriorization of your physical conditions.

Get warm and dry. Bail out the raft or boat. Wring the water out of your clothes. Give what dry clothing or blankets as can be afforded to those who are injured or excessively cold or wet, and help them warm themselves. Protect them from wind and spray as much as possible.

Hand out motion sickness medicine. This seemingly trivial precaution should not be ignored. Bobbing around in a small boat or raft can cause seasickness of such severity that it incapacitates even the saltiest crew, leaving them unable to care for themselves or even assist in their own rescue for days at a time. For those who *are* sick, fresh air and an opportunity to look at the horizon awhile may also help.

Prevent sunburn. If it is sunny, and sunscreen lotion is available, see that it is used. Severe sunburn can occur quickly and unexpectedly on the water, so guard against it carefully.

Keep a record. Open a log beginning with your present position as nearly as can be established. In it you should record all items of navigational or legal interest, such as estimated positions, fixes, names of all aboard, injuries, deaths, and burials at sea.

Take stock of the crew. Assess the physical condition and capabilities of each individual. This will keep you from missing some not-so-apparent injuries, and the information will also be useful later on when you start assigning various duties.

Inventory your food, water, and provisions. Set up a rationing system. If you are on a raft rather than a boat, your survival will probably depend mainly on your ability to wait the situation out. Plan accordingly.

If you feel, however, that land is within your sailing range, base your rationing system on the expected number of days till arrival. But be conservative. In any case, no one should eat or drink during the first 24 hours. And no matter how long you expect to be stranded or how thirsty you are, do not drink sea water.

Rig a radar reflector. Many survival kits already include a corner reflector. If yours does not, one may be made from metallic debris. Aluminum foil, sheet metal, or a jerry can (with the sides dented in) hoisted overhead should do quite satisfactorily. Keep it as high as possible.

Join up with other rafts. Rafts are more likely to be noticed if they stay close together, and they also may be able to provide mutual support. Tie them to each other with twenty- or thirty-foot pieces of line to minimize strain.

Travel or Wait?

Early on in your ordeal, you will have to decide whether to stay and await rescue or to strike out for safe haven. And if you decide to travel, a destination and route must be chosen. These decisions may prove difficult, and there are a number of factors that should be weighed carefully against one another before a final course of action is selected.

If there was an opportunity to send out a good distress signal before abandoning your mother craft, the chances are pretty fair that searchers will be arriving soon at the point where the transmission was made. In this case, it would probably be best just to throw out a sea anchor, make yourselves as highly visible as possible, set a good lookout, and wait. If searchers do not arrive within two or three days, reevaluate. Also, if you are near commercial shipping lanes, there would be doubtful advantage gained by travel if it would take you away from them, (unless, of course, you are very close to land).

Other factors to consider are winds, currents, and motive power available, and the accuracy with which you feel navigation can be accomplished.

If you decide to head for refuge, the land mass that is closest may *not* be the wisest destination to choose. One might be wiser, for instance, to try for a continental land mass 1,000 miles to leeward instead of a small island 100 miles up wind. (Or perhaps it would be better to head for, or at least detour through, commercial shipping lanes if any are nearby.)

As a source of propulsion for traveling any real distance, sail power is by far the best, and ocean currents are a close second.

It may be difficult, if not impossible, to go in any direction but directly downwind with a jury-rigged sail (especially if you are in a rubber raft), but even the longest range small craft can go only a couple of hundred miles on a full load of fuel. And the use of paddles or oars will exhaust the crew in no time.

So, be patient and stick with sail power even if you have to concoct your rig out of dungarees and swab handles. And if the wind is absent or just weak and going in the worst possible direction, but the currents are headed the right way, don't forget that a sea anchor can actually help you along by catching more of the deeper current. Save your fuel and energy for making your approach and landing when you reach the coast. If there is any kind of surf on the beach you select, you will probably need them.

Lifeboat Navigation

The navigation of a lifeboat across open ocean is a stiff challenge to the mettle of a man and his resourcefulness. It requires a thorough understanding of wind and current in addition to a sound foundation in the principles of mathematics, piloting, and celestial mechanics. Hundreds of pages have been written on this subject alone, and in a text of this nature, it is not practical to offer more than some helpful ideas and advice upon which the individual already well grounded in the art of navigation may build. The following information should get the potential navigator thinking along the right lines, and those interested in a more "in depth" discussion will find a wealth of knowledge in the references listed in the bibliography.

Instruments and Aids

You will find that the "what to take" list at the end of this chapter includes an "electronic slide rule"-type calculator and a sextant. Far from being an extravagant investment, at the time of this writing an inexpensive but perfectly satisfactory model of each can be purchased for under $25.00. A sextant in this price range will probably not be accurate to better than about two minutes of arc (or about two miles at the equator) but any finer accuracy is unnecessary for our present purposes.

A portable radio receiver is also included on the list. Although probably more expensive than the above items, a small battery-powered multiband unit could prove invaluable for receiving time signals, maritime communications, weather information, or even for use as a direction finder. If one is available, take it along.

Chart. The best types of charts to carry are Pilot Charts, for not only are they of a manageable scale, but they also contain important wind and current data.

Dead reckoning track. A carefully kept DR track will probably be your most dependable navigation asset. It can be plotted on a chart, derived graphically, or calculated mathematically. A set of traverse tables should be helpful if you are using the last of these three methods. Remember that wind and current will have a proportionally much greater effect on your small craft than they have on a fast-moving ship.

Speed measurement. To measure your boat's speed through the water, toss something lightweight and expendable—such as a wood chip—overboard at the bow, and time it as it passes down the side. To make the calculations easier, mark off the gunwale in five- or ten-foot intervals. One hundred feet per minute equals one knot. If you would like to reuse the chip, just tie one end of a piece of small stuff to it, and tie the other end to the stern of the boat. Then, when you have timed it, just haul the chip back aboard.

Time. If a watch with a second hand is not available for measuring time, seconds may be approximated by counting "one thousand, two thousand, etc." For greater accuracy, a pendulum can be used. A pendulum 39.1 inches long (measured to the center of the weight) will have a period of two seconds. (The period is the time required for one full swing, over and back.)

The problem of time measurement has plagued navigators for centuries, the biggest problem it presented being that of finding one's longitude. This, however, is not so great a problem as it once was, for the average man now may routinely carry an electronic timepiece that functions with less error than many ships' chronometers of only a few years back. But whether or not one of these is available, every timepiece aboard should be collected, wound as appropriate, and have its error established as nearly as possible. Then all should be stored upright in a dry, watertight container, and the ones that require winding should be wound regularly.

Reference information. A little selected information copied from a navigation text or almanac will help make your job easier and your success greater. For instance, tables for altitude corrections, equation of time, and traverse traveling are nearly indispensable and take very little time to record. Even an entire long-term almanac (as is contained in Appendix H of *Bowditch* Vol. II, 1975) and selected extracts from Appendixes F and G (altitude corrections) require only a few pages, and are well worth the effort required to pack them with your emergency gear.

A jury-rigged sextant. If you find yourself without a sextant, a fair substitute may be constructed using a protractor, maneuvering board, or plotting sheet, and a string with a weight. Attach the weight to one end of the string and fasten the other end to the center of the protractor/maneuvering board as illustrated in figure 17. To ascertain the altitude of a body, sight along the top edge of the instrument, lock the string in place with your finger, and read the altitude from beneath the string.

Fixes with no sextant. Even with no altitude-measuring device at all, fixes may still be taken by observing and recording the time of rise or set for various bodies and calculating a line of position using an observed altitude of zero. Because of the in-

64 SEAMANSHIP

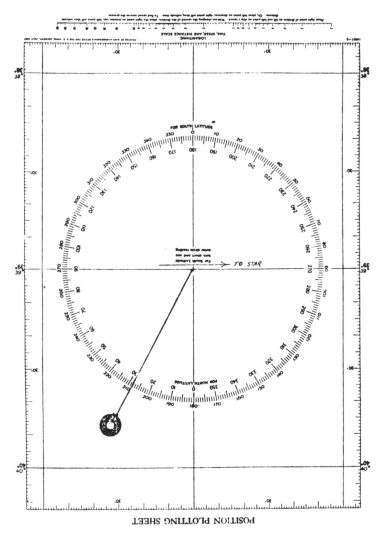

Figure 17. Makeshift sextant

herent inaccuracy of observations taken near the horizon, all correction factors must be meticulously applied for this method to succeed.

Latitude sailing. Do not be discouraged if you have difficulty determining your longitude. Many seamen have circumnavigated the world without a dependable means of finding it. They traveled by latitude sailing, and unless your destination is a continent-sized land mass, it might be wise to follow their example. Simply stated, "latitude sailing" means sailing to a point somewhere short of, but on the same latitude as, your destination; then, once the latitude is reached, you sail directly east or west along that line of latitude toward your goal until you arrive. By using this method you avoid the need to depend on longitude calculations, and although it may add some miles to the journey, it is a nearly foolproof scheme for hitting your target on the first try.

Latitude by Polaris. A simple but dependable method of finding one's latitude in the Northern Hemisphere without the use of an almanac or timepiece is by observing the North Star, Polaris.

The star Polaris is located approximately 1° from the north celestial pole. Therefore, its altitude, plus or minus the appropriate correction of 1° or less, is equal to the latitude of the observer. The necessary correction can easily be estimated by noting the angle of the Big Dipper relative to the vertical.

If a line is drawn from Polaris to Alkaid, the star at the tip of the Big Dipper's handle, it passes almost directly through the north celestial pole. (Remember, the altitude of the celestial pole is exactly equal to the observer's latitude.) Obviously, if our imaginary line is horizontal, there will be no difference between the altitude of Polaris and the celestial pole. The correction will be zero. If the line is vertical, however, the difference in altitudes will be at its maximum of about 1° (added if Alkaid is above Polaris and subtracted if it is below). A usable correction for a position between these two extremes can be approximated by simple interpolation. (See figure 18.)

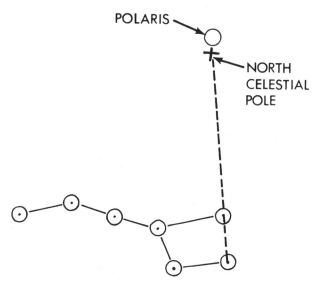

Figure 18. Polaris and the north celestial pole

Direction by Orion. Another handy navigational aid is the constellation Orion, because of the singular position it occupies in the night sky. The star Mintaka, which is the northernmost star in Orion's belt, lies directly on the celestrial equator. (See figure 19.) Therefore, this star rises exactly on a true bearing of 270° (due west) no matter what the observer's location on the earth's surface. This information would be especially handy to someone stranded in the Southern Hemisphere, where the North Star is unavailable for direction finding.

Direction from a timepiece. Holding a properly set and running watch on its back, turn it so that the hour hand points toward the sun. Now imagine a line drawn from the "12" to the clock's center. An arrow bisecting the angle made by the hour hand and this line will point due south in the Northern Hemisphere, and due north in the Southern Hemisphere. (See figure 20.)

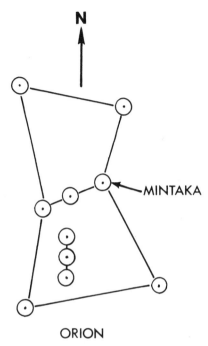

ORION

Figure 19. Orion

What to Take

It is the responsibility of the first lieutenant to ensure that the lifeboats and rafts are properly equipped. Article 640 of the *Standard Operations and Regulations Manual* lists the required gear and equipment, and these tables may be found in Appendix C. In addition to the gear required by regulation, the following items are also recommended for inclusion in an "abandon ship" packet.

- Notebook
- Pencils/pens and erasers
- Bible
- Clothing and blankets

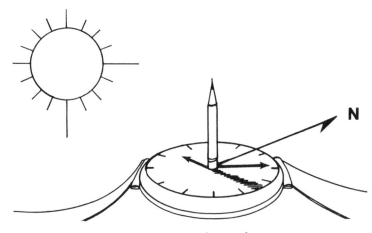

Figure 20. Direction from the sun and a watch

- Sunglasses
- Sunscreen lotion
- Magnetic compass
- Watch or clock
- Protractor
- Charts of the area (preferably Pilot Charts)
- Sextant
- *Nautical Almanac*
- Navigation tables and star charts or a copy of *Bowditch*
- "Electronic slide rule" calculator (with extra batteries)
- Graph paper
- Dividers/drafting compass
- Pad of maneuvering boards
- Portable radio
- Flares
- Firearm and ammunition

First Aid

The purpose of first aid is to provide *immediate* but *temporary* treatment for a victim of injury or sudden illness until professional medical assistance can be obtained. Note the key words immediate and temporary. It is important that proper first aid be administered quickly and efficiently when needed, but it is equally if not more important that the victim be afforded the services of trained medical personnel at the earliest possible moment.

Since improper treatment can be worse than no treatment at all, it is imperative that the initial actions taken be the right ones. The following list of "Dos" and "Don'ts" may help the potential rescuer make the correct decisions if and when the need arises.

The Dos

- Act promptly but *calmly*.
- *Reassure* the victim and at the same time quickly and gently examine him to determine the need for lifesaving measures.
Vital action: Stop severe (deadly) bleeding.

Open the airway and restore breathing and heartbeat. If required, take the above actions instantly.

- *Reexamine* the victim immediately in a careful, gentle, organized (head to toe, front to back) manner to determine if there are any other injuries, and render treatment if required.
Vital action: Prevent shock (put his feet up, keep him warm and calm).

Dress and bandage wounds (to avoid infection), and splint broken bones.

- Note again the order of vital actions: stop severe bleeding; restore breathing and heartbeat; prevent shock; dress, bandage, and splint.

Don'ts

- Do not remove the victim's clothing by pulling or tearing it. Cut it away.
- Do not touch or try to clean a dirty wound, including burns.
- Do not remove dressings and bandages once they have been placed over a wound.

- Do not loosen a tourniquet once it has been applied.
- Do not give fluids by mouth to someone who is unconscious, extremely nauseated, or vomiting, or who has an abdominal or neck wound.
- Do not move a victim who has a fracture until it has been properly splinted, unless it is dangerous for him to remain where he is.
- Do not position the victim on his back if he is unconscious or has a face or neck wound.
- Do not permit the head of a victim with a head injury to be lower than his body.
- Do not give morphine to a victim of a head wound or to someone who is unconscious.
- Do not try to push protruding intestines or brain tissue back into a wound (unless it is necessary in order to cover the wound adequately.) Just apply sterile dressings over them.
- Do not put any medication on a burn.
- Do not leave a sucking chest wound unsealed. Have the victim exhale forcibly and hold his breath while you seal and dress it with petroleum gauze, a plastic dressing wrapper, or some other airtight material.
- Do not administer first aid measures that are unnecessary or beyond your capabilities.

3 Piloting

Rules of the Road

The Rules of the Road, both International and Inland, delineate maneuvering signals, danger signals, emergency and distress signals, low visibility signals, steering rules, and lights and shapes to be used by all vessels on waters under their jurisdiction.

The International Rules must be obeyed by all public and private vessels while navigating on "the high seas and in all waters connected therewith navigable by seagoing vessels" and in any other waters not otherwise governed by special regulation. They were established with the agreement and consent of the world's maritime nations and became effective in the United States in 1977 by passage of an act of Congress.

Inland Rules of the Road, supplemented primarily by the Pilot Rules, are to be obeyed by all vessels navigating certain areas along the coasts, in the ocean harbors, and in the coastal rivers of the United States and her possessions (with certain specific exceptions). They are federal statutes and hold the full impact of federal law in every sense.

The exceptions to the Inland Rules' jurisdiction are the Great Lakes and their connecting and tributary waters as far east as Montreal; the Mississippi River above Huey P. Long Bridge, and all the Mississippi tributaries and their tributaries; the Atchafalaya River above its junction with the Plaquemine-Morgan City Alternate Waterway; and the Red River of the North. The above waters have special rules duly made by local authority.

Maneuvering Rules

Under the Inland and International Rules of the Road, all situations involving risk of collision between two vessels may be classified as meeting, crossing, or overtaking situations, and the law gives specific instructions to be followed by both vessels in each case. (Risk of collision should be considered to exist whenever two vessels pass near enough to each other that departure from the Rules by either craft could result in a collision.)

Under the Rules, the relationships of vessels that will pass in close proximity to each other are expressed in terms of their stand-on or give-way status. The give-way vessel is defined as the vessel upon which the responsibility for avoiding collision rests. It is up to her to make the necessary course and speed changes to pass clear of the stand-on vessel.

The primary responsibility of the stand-on vessel is to hold her course and speed until all risk of collision is past, thereby making it possible for the other vessel to plan her avoidance maneuvers intelligently. This responsibility exists for the stand-on vessel until an "in extremis" situation is reached. If an in extremis situation does evolve, the top priority of both vessels should be to make whatever maneuvers are necessary to minimize or eliminate the imminent collision. (In extremis is best defined as a situation in which *both* ships *must* maneuver if a collision is to be avoided.)

If at any time a vessel is not sure as to whether she is in a stand-on or give-way status, she should consider herself to be in a give-way status and maneuver accordingly.

The three possible situations that involve risk of collision and the appropriate maneuvering alternatives are summarized in table 8.

Crossing, overtaking, and meeting situations are defined by the following circumstances (see figures 21, 22, and 23).

Crossing

A crossing situation exists when two ships in sight of one another are approaching approximately the same point although perhaps

Table 8. Maneuvering Rules

Situation	Give-way Vessel	Maneuvering Alternatives for the Give-way Vessel[1]	Maneuvering Alternatives for the Stand-on Vessel[1]
Crossing	Port vessel (vessel which has the other on her starboard side)	Come starboard and/or slow or stop until risk of collision is passed. Come left only under exceptional circumstances.	Hold course and speed until risk of collision is passed or until extremis is reached or until it becomes apparent that the other vessel is not taking sufficient or appropriate action under the Rules.
Overtaking	Overtaking vessel (vessel which has the other ahead or on her bow)	Come left to pass other vessel on her port side (preferred action). Come starboard to pass other vessel on her starboard side (Less preferred action). Turn away and/ or slow down to completely avoid passing the other vessel.	Hold course and speed until risk of collision is passed or until extremis is reached or until it becomes apparent that the other vessel is not taking sufficient or appropriate action under the Rules.
Meeting	Both vessels are give-way (burdened)	Both vessels come starboard so that each passes the other on her port side. Vessels should pass to starboard only if they can do so without altering course and will pass at such a distance that the risk of collision cannot exist.	Neither vessel has stand-on status.

[1] Should be accompanied by the appropriate whistle signal.

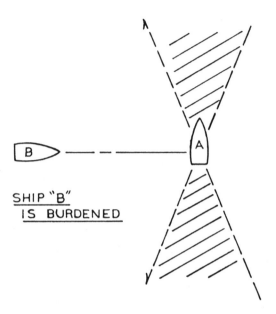

Figure 21. Crossing

not to arrive at the same time, and they are not in a meeting or an overtaking situation.

Overtaking

An overtaking situation exists when one vessel is approaching another from a direction more than 22.5 degrees abaft her beam, that is, in such a position with reference to the vessel she is overtaking that at night she would be able to see only the sternlight of that vessel but neither of her side-lights.

Meeting (Head-on)

A meeting situation exists when two vessels are meeting on reciprocal or nearly reciprocal courses so as to involve risk of collision. Such a situation should be deemed to exist when a vessel sees the other ahead or nearly ahead and by night she

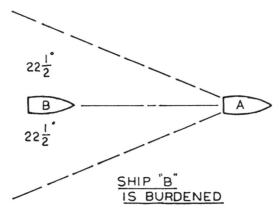

Figure 22. Overtaking

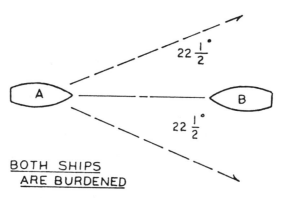

Figure 23. Meeting

could see the masthead lights of the other in a line or nearly in a line or both side-lights and by day she sees the corresponding aspect of the other vessel.

Right-of-Way Priority List

The following is a priority list (or "ticking order") of right of way for vessels that are of different types and have varying degrees of maneuverability. Any vessel on this list has right of way over any vessels listed below it and is burdened to keep out of the way of any vessel listed above it. This "ticking order" has priority over all other maneuvering or right-of-way rules except the "overtaking" rule, and it, of course, may not apply in situations involving special circumstances as defined under the Rules or in the case of the exceptions named at the end of the list. This order is established by the International Rules of the Road, and of the cases listed, the Inland Rules address only the right of way of sailing vessels over steam vessels, and of fishing vessels over sailing vessels. However, even in Inland waters, the wise boatman will find this a useful guide to the relative maneuverability of the vessels listed, and will see that his craft is handled accordingly.

1. Vessel not under command.

2. Vessel restricted in ability to maneuver.

3. Vessel engaged in fishing.

4. Sailing vessel under sail.

5. Power-driven vessel under way and not constrained by abnormal circumstances.

Exceptions. Vessels less than 20 meters (International Rules) or 65 feet (Inland Rules) in length, sailing vessels, and vessels engaged in fishing must not impede the safe passage of any other vessel navigating within a narrow channel or fairway, or following a traffic lane.

Maneuvering Signals

Table 9 lists and explains the various maneuvering signals that are mandatory for all vessels under the International and Inland Rules of the Road. It is important to note that International whistle signals indicate actions that are already being taken, while whistle signals under the Inland Rules are primarily expressions of intent and acknowledgment of intent to carry out certain maneuvers. In addition, the Inland Rules *require* an *exchange* of identical signals to ensure that both vessels agree on a course of action before it is carried out. All the signals,

Table 9. Whistle Signals

Signal	Meaning
International Rules	
One short blast	I am altering course to starboard
Two short blasts	I am altering course to port
Three short blasts	My engines are backing
Five short blasts	Danger signal
One prolonged blast	I am approaching a blind bend in the channel
short blast = one second in duration	
prolonged blast = four to six seconds in duration	
Inland Rules	
One short blast	I propose a port-to-port passage
Two short blasts	I propose a stbd-to-stbd passage
Three short blasts	My engines are backing
Four short blasts	a) What are your intentions
	b) There is danger in the maneuver
	c) I don't agree with your proposal
One long blast	I am approaching a blind bend in the channel
short blast = one second in duration	
long blast = eight to ten seconds in duration	

with the exceptions of the long or prolonged blast for vessels approaching a blind bend, and the four-short-blast danger signal, are only for use by vessels that are in sight of one another.

Restricted Visibility

Restricted visibility signals should be sounded whenever visibility is impaired to a degree that it may interfere with safe navigation. Although they are often called fog signals, their use is not limited exclusively to fog conditions. They are also mandatory for vessels in or *near* heavy rain, snow, mist, haze, or any other such vision-limiting phenomena. Table 10 lists and defines the applicable Inland and International signals.

When navigating under less than optimum conditions of visibility, remember that no matter what the visibility range is, half of it "belongs to the other guy." Accordingly, speed should be restricted to the point that your vessel can be completely stopped within a distance that is equal to, or less than, half the visibility range.

Whenever there is any question as to the location, course, speed, or danger of collision presented by another vessel, you should proceed with utmost caution, slowing or stopping the engines if necessary, until the problem is resolved.

Lights and Shapes for Vessels

In addition to maneuvering rules and signals, the Inland and International Rules of the Road also specify various lights and

Table 10. **Fog (Low Visibility) Signals**

International			Inland	
Signal	Maximum Interval	Situation	Signal	Maximum Interval
-	2 Min.	Power-driven vessel or steam vessel u/w with way on	-	1 Min.
- -	2 Min.	Power-driven vessel u/w but no way on	-	1 Min.
- . .	2 Min.	Vessel not under command Vessel restricted in her ability to maneuver Vessel constrained by her draft Vessel engaged in fishing		
		Vessel engaged in towing or pushing another vessel ahead	- . .	1 Min.
		Sailing vessel on starboard tack	0	1 Min.
		Sailing vessel on port tack	0 0	1 Min.
		Sailng vessel with wind abaft the beam	0 0 0	1 Min.
- . . .	2 Min.	Vessel towed	- . .	1 Min.
-	2 Min.	Composite unit u/w with way on		
- -	2 Min.	Composite unit u/w with no way on		
X	1 Min.	Vessel at anchor	X	1 Min.

Table 10. Fog (Low Visibility) Signals (Cont.)

International			Inland	
Signal	Maximum Interval	Situation	Signal	Maximum Interval
. - .		Additional sound signal that an anchored vessel may sound when a dangerous situation seems to be developing	None	
3 X 3	1 Min.	Vessel aground	None	
None		All rafts or other water craft not provided for, navigating by hand power, horse power, current of the river	0	1 Min.
. . . .		Pilot vessel when engaged on pilotage duty may give this identity signal	None	

- Represents a prolonged blast. (about four to six seconds)
. Represents a short blast. (about one second)
0 Represents a blast. (duration unspecified)
3 Represents three strokes on the bell.
X Represents rapidly ringing the bell for 5 seconds and on vessels of 100 meters or longer in international waters rapidly ringing a gong in the aft part of the vessel for 5 seconds after the bell.

shapes to be displayed by vessels to signify the functions they perform, or their method of operation. The illustrations in this section (figures 24 through 29) are by no means all-inclusive, but they do show the primary configurations to be observed under the International Rules. The lights should be displayed from sunset to sunrise and any other time visibility is restricted, and the dayshapes should be displayed during all daylight hours. (*Note*: Small craft are permitted by Public Law 552 of the 84th Congress to display the navigational lights required for international waters in both inland and international waters. This means that only the international navigational lights are needed by small craft since these lights can be used in both national and international waters.)

Figure 24. Power-driven vessel, 50 meters and upward, under way

Figure 25. Vessel constrained by draft

Aids to Navigation

This section summarizes the primary buoyage systems and components in use throughout the world and of interest to the small craft sailor. These aids to navigation consist of fixed or floating structures that have differing degrees of reliability—with some marks likely to be missing, shifted, overturned, extinguished, damaged, or otherwise not properly located, visible, or audible.

Buoys

Buoys may take many different forms, varying from small plastic spheres less than a foot in diameter to large navigational buoys over forty feet across. Later in this chapter there is further discussion of buoy types and uses, as buoyage systems are described.

The prudent mariner will remember that, due to inherent inaccuracies in placing and maintaining a buoy in exact location,

Figure 26. Power-driven vessel 50 meters and upward towing astern. Length of tow greater than 200 meters.

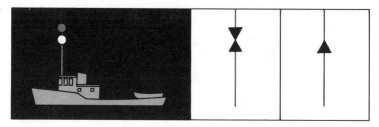

Figure 27. Vessel engaged in fishing (under way or at anchor)

buoy positions shown on charts are only approximate. Any buoy, therefore, should be passed with a wide safety margin where possible. Otherwise, one may be in danger not only of striking a yawing buoy or its mooring chain, but also of colliding with the obstruction that the buoy may mark.

Lights for Buoys and Other Navigation Aids

Lights are given distinctive characteristics both to distinguish one from another, and also to convey certain definite information. This distinctiveness is obtained by employing lights of various colors, lights that burn steadily, and others that flash at intervals. By varying the periods of the light and darkness of any of the flashing or occulting cycles, a variety of characteristics may be obtained. Light Lists, local charts, and other pertinent references will provide detailed explanations and de-

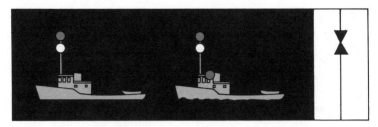

Figure 28. Vessel engaged in trawling—not making way (left), making way (right)

Figure 29. Vessel at anchor

scriptions of the lights in use in any particular area. The diagrams in Appendix H include the meanings of some various light characteristics and codes.

Colored Light Sectors

Sectors of colored glass or plastic are placed in the lanterns of certain lights to mark shoals and to warn mariners off the nearby land. Lights so equipped show one color from most directions and a different color or colors over definite arcs of the horizon as indicated in the Light Lists and upon the charts. A sector changes the color of a light when viewed from certain directions, but not the characteristic. For example, a flashing white light having a red sector will appear flashing red when viewed from within the sector.

Sectors may be but a few degrees in width, marking an isolated rock or shoal, or of such width as to extend from the direction of the deep water toward shore. Bearings referring to sectors are expressed in degrees as observed from a vessel toward the light.

In the majority of cases, water areas covered by red sectors should be avoided, the exact extent of the danger being determined from an examination of the charts. In some cases a narrow sector may mark the best water across a shoal. A narrow sector may also mark a turning point in a channel.

Identification of Lights

The charts, and the *Light List* or *List of Lights* as published by the Coast Guard should be consulted to learn the exact characteristics of the lights that are expected to be seen. When a light is observed, note its color, and by means of a watch or clock with a second hand, note the time required for the light to perform its full cycle of changes. If color, cycle, and number of flashes per cycle agree with the information on the chart or the Lists, you have made a correct identification. Most lighted aids to navigation are automatically extinguished during daylight hours by switches activated by daylight. These switches are not of equal sensitivity, therefore all lights do not come on or go off at the same time.

The Lists should be examined to ascertain if any other light in the general locality may be seen and mistaken for the desired light. If there is a doubt, careful timing of all flashes and dark intervals for comparison with the Light Lists is usually conclusive.

Light Structures

Lighted aids to navigation vary from the tallest lighthouse on the coast flashing with millions of candlepower, to a simple battery-powered lantern on a wooden pile in a small creek. Light structures are established in positions where they function more suitably than buoys. They serve the same functions, and with the exception of lighthouses, they generally have the same numbering, coloring, and light and sound characteristics as buoys.

Lighthouses are placed where they will be of most use; on prominent headlands, at entrances, on isolated dangers, or at other points where it is necessary to warn or guide mariners. Their principal purpose is to support a light at a considerable height above the water. In many instances, fog signals, radio-beacon equipment, and automatic apparatuses are housed in separate buildings located near the tower.

Lightships serve the same purpose as lighthouses, being equipped with lights, fog signals, and radio beacons. Ships are used only because they must be placed at points where it has been impracticable to build lighthouses.

With advanced technology, all lightships but one have been replaced with light towers, large navigational buoys (LNBs), or other such structures in the United States.

Daymarks

Daymarks, signboards atop minor aids to navigation, serve to make them readily visible and easily identifiable in daylight, and they convey to the mariner the significance that lights do at night. For example, the distinctive painted pattern on a light-house serves to identify the light during the day. The same is true for a minor light structure, which may be merely a lantern on a single pile; it is identified during the day by the coloring and shape of its daymarks.

Daymarks are also used on structures without lights. Such aids are called *daybeacons* and often serve as range, warning, or regulatory markers, in addition to being used as channel or obstruction avoidance aids. They are usually covered with reflective material. Appendix H includes illustrations of daymarks.

Ranges

Ranges are two structures which, when appearing to be in line (i.e., one over the other), indicate to the mariner that he is on a safe course. They can be either lighted or unlighted.

By steering a course that keeps these structures in line (see figure 30), the mariner will remain within the confines of the

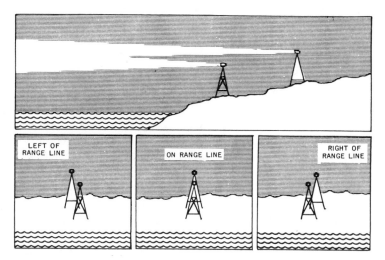

Figure 30. Range lights

channel. Remember: ranges cannot be used for the entire time
you can see them. Quite a few of them are on shore, and that's
where you will be if you don't consult your chart as to where
to change course.

Fog Signals

Most lighthouses and lightships and some minor light structures
and buoys are equipped with sound-producing instruments to
aid the mariner in periods of low visibility. Charts and the Light
Lists of the particular area should be consulted for positive
identification. Caution: buoys fitted with a bell, gong, or whistle
and actuated by wave motion may produce no sound when the
sea is calm. Their positive identification is not always possible.

Any sound-producing instrument operated in time of fog from
a definite point shown on the charts, such as a lighthouse,
lightship, or buoy, serves as a useful fog signal. To be effective
as an aid to navigation, a mariner must be able to identify it
and to know from what point it is sounded. At all lighthouses

and lightships equipped with fog signals, these signals are operated by mechanical or electrical means and are sounded during periods of low visibility, providing the desirable feature of positive identification.

The characteristics of mechanized signals are varied blasts and silent periods. A definite time is required for each signal to perform a complete cycle. Where the number of blasts and the total time for a signal to complete a cycle is not sufficient for positive identification, reference may be made to details in the Light Lists regarding the exact length of each blast and silent interval. The various types of fog signals also differ in tone, and this facilitates recognition of the respective stations.

Buoyage Systems

With modifications, two primary systems of buoyage are in general use throughout the world. These are the lateral system and the cardinal system.

In the lateral system, the location of each buoy indicates the direction of the danger it marks relative to the course that should normally be followed. Thus, a buoy that should be kept on the port hand lies between the vessel and the danger when the buoy is abeam to port, approximately.

In principle, the positions of marks in the lateral system are determined by the general direction taken by the mariner when approaching a harbor, river, estuary, or other waterway from seaward, and may also be determined with reference to the main stream of flood current. The application of this principle is defined, as required, by nautical documents such as *Sailing Directions*.

Under the cardinal system, the location of each buoy indicates the approximate true bearing of the danger it marks. Thus, an eastern quadrant buoy marks a danger, such as a shoal, that lies to the west of the buoy, approximately.

Although almost all of the major maritime nations have used either the lateral or the cardinal system for many years, details such as the shapes and colors of the buoys, and the characteristics and colors of lighted aids generally have varied from country to country. Differences in the various methods as applied to the cardinal system are comparatively slight, but two distinct methods of applying the lateral system have evolved. The major discrepancy has been in the colors of the buoys and of their lights.

The Technical Committee of the International Association of Lighthouse Authorities (IALA), a nongovernmental body that brings together representatives of aids to navigation based on the latest technology, has decided that a single worldwide system of buoyage cannot be achieved at present, but considers that the use of only two alternative systems is practicable. The two systems are termed: IALA Maritime Buoyage System "A"— Combined Cardinal and Lateral System (Red to Port); IALA Maritime Buoyage System "B"—Lateral System only (Red to Starboard).

While System "B" is still being studied, the rules of System "A" have been completed and have the support of the Intergovernmental Maritime Consultative Organization (IMCO). Implementation of System "A" began in the waters of northwest Europe in 1977.

It is expected that the following countries will adopt System "A":

Belgium
Denmark
Federal Republic of Germany (West)
France
German Democractic Republic (East)
Netherlands
Norway
Poland
Republic of Ireland
Sweden
United Kingdom
U.S.S.R.

Uniform System (See Appendix H)

As recommended by the League of Nations in 1936, a country uses the *Uniform Lateral System* (Red to Port) or the *Uniform Cardinal System*, or both, according to its requirements or preference. When both are used, the transition from one to the other must be clearly indicated in appropriate publications, such as *Sailing Directions*, or by suitable buoyage marks.

Both the Uniform Lateral System and the Uniform Cardinal System employ topmarks as an additional means of identification. Unless otherwise stated in the appendix, a topmark is painted the darker of the colors used on the buoy. In the Uniform Cardinal System, they are optional in every case except on wreck buoys.

In both the Uniform Lateral System and the Uniform Cardinal System, lighted buoys have the same shape as the unlighted buoys shown.

In both the Uniform Lateral System and the Uniform Cardinal System, a quick-flashing light is regarded as a single flashing light.

The numbering or lettering of fairway and channel buoys is an optional feature of the Uniform Lateral System. In the United States System these buoys are always numbered, commencing from seaward.

IALA Maritime Buoyage System "A"—Combined Cardinal and Lateral System (Red to Port)

System "A" (see Appendix H) applies to all fixed and floating marks—other than lighthouses, sector lights, leading lights and marks, lightships, and large navigational buoys (lighthouse buoys)—and serves to indicate:
- The sides and centerlines of navigable channels.
- Natural dangers and other obstructions, such as wrecks.
- Areas in which navigation may be subject to regulation.
- Other features of importance to the mariner.

It should be understood that most lighted and unlighted beacons, other than leading marks, are included in the system. In general, beacon topmarks will have the same shape and colors as those used on buoys.

The system provides *five types of marks* that may be used in any combination:

 • Lateral marks, which indicate the port and starboard sides of channels.

 • Cardinal marks, used in conjunction with the compass, which indiate that the navigable water lies to the named side of the mark.

 • Isolated danger marks, which are erected on, or moored directly on or over, dangers of limited extent.

 • Safe-water marks, such as mid-channel buoys.

 • Special marks, the purpose of which is apparent from reference to the chart or other nautical documents.

Marks currently used that will be superseded by System "A" include those that indicate wrecks, middle grounds, secondary channels, bifurcations, and junctions; there are no special "landfall" or "transition" marks in System "A". There is no differentiation between the marks for such special features as spoil grounds, anchorages, cable areas, and military exercise areas, all of which will be marked by yellow buoys—which may, in addition, carry lettering to indicate the purpose of the buoy.

The significance of a mark depends on one or more features:

 • *By day*—color, shape, and topmark.

 • *By night*—light color and phase characteristics.

Red and green (without stripes or bands) are reserved, respectively, for port and starboard lateral marks, and yellow for special marks. The other types of marks have horizontal bands or vertical stripes.

There are *five basic buoy shapes*, namely, can, conical, spherical, pillar, and spar. In the case of can, conical and spherical, the shape indicates the correct side to pass. With pillar and spar buoys, the shape has no special significance.

The term "pillar" is used to describe any buoy that is smaller than a "lighthouse buoy" and has a tall, central structure on a broad base; it includes beacon buoys, high-focal-plane buoys, and others (except spar buoys), whose body shape does not indicate the correct side to pass.

It must be understood that much existing equipment will be used in the new system—including, for example, light-floats. Variations on the basic shapes will therefore be fairly common, but by day, the colors and topmarks should prevent ambiguity.

System "A" makes use of can, conical, spherical, and X-shaped topmarks only. Topmarks on pillar and spar buoys are particularly important and will be used wherever practicable, but ice or other severe conditions may occasionally prevent their use.

Where marks are lighted, red and green lights are reserved, respectively, for port and starboard lateral marks, and yellow for special marks. The other types of marks have a white light, distinguished one from another by phase characteristic.

Red and green lights may have any phase characteristic, as the color alone is sufficient to show on which side they should be passed. Special marks, when lighted, have a yellow light with any phase characteristic not reserved for white lights of the system. The other types of marks have clearly specified phase characteristics of white light: various quick-flashing phase characteristics for cardinal marks, group flashing (2) for isolated danger marks, and relatively long periods of light for safe-water marks.

Single fixed lights (often found on shore marks at present) are being discontinued in the United Kingdom because of the possibility of confusion with ships' lights.

United States System (See Appendix H)

The waters of the United States are marked by the lateral system of buoyage (red markers to starboard, black to port) recommended by the International Marine Conference of 1889. As all channels do not lead from seaward, arbitrary assumptions are at times made in order that the system may be consistently applied. Along the sea coasts of the United States, the characteristics are based upon the assumption that proceeding "from seaward" constitutes a *clock-wise* direction: a southerly direction along the Gulf Coast, and a northerly direction along the Pacific Coast. On the Great Lakes, a westerly and northerly direction is taken as being "from seaward" (except on Lake Michigan, where a southerly direction is used). On the Mississippi and Ohio Rivers and their tributaries, the characteristics of aids to navigation are determined as proceeding from sea toward the head of navigation. On the Intracoastal Waterway, proceeding in a generally southerly direction along the Atlantic Coast and in a generally westerly direction along the Gulf Coast is considered as proceeding "from seaward."

The continuation of the lateral system along the coasts in the order indicated refers only to the side of the vessel on which buoys are to be kept, as indicated by color, shape, and light, if any; there is no numerical continuity between coastal buoys. In fairways and channels, however, buoys are numbered consecutively from seaward, even numbers to starboard, odd to port.

In the United States system, lighted buoys, bell buoys, whistle buoys, and combination buoys may differ in shape from the unlighted buoys shown in Appendix H, but not in color or marking.

The United States system of buoyage is supplemented by various additional shapes and colors along the Intracoastal Waterway and under the Uniform State Waterway Marking System. These supplemental marks are illustrated in Appendix H.

Memory aids. Mariners have long used the following two memory aids (or approximate variants thereof) for piloting in United States coastal waters:

● Even red nuns carry odd black cans. (The red buoys will be nuns (conical buoys) and are always *even* numbered. The buoys on the opposite side of the channel will be black can buoys having *odd* numbers.)

● Red, right, returning. (Red buoys will be left on your *right*, or starboard side, when *returning* from the sea.

(*Note*: In early 1980, the U.S. Coast Guard began experimenting with the use of *green* buoys in place of *black* ones with a view to increasing the visibility of the buoys. If the experiments are successful, a gradual shift to *green* port channel markers may be expected.)

4 Boat Etiquette and Insignia

Etiquette

The observance of military etiquette, customs, and courtesy in ships' boats is tantamount in importance to your social etiquette ashore in evaluating and establishing your deportment. The primary points to which an officer should give his attention are explained below.

Salutes and honors shall be exchanged as indicated in the following paragraphs.

The junior shall always salute first and the senior shall return the salute with the hand. Seniority of a boat is established by the rank of the senior officer aboard her. If a doubt exists about the rank of an officer in a boat, it is better to salute than to risk neglecting to salute one entitled to that courtesy. The coxswain or boat officer, if present, rises to deliver or receive salutes. The rest of the crew stands at attention. Passengers sit at attention. Sitting at attention in a boat is sitting erect.

In laden boats, towing boats, or boats under sail, make only the hand salute on any occasion.

If a boat is carrying a person for whom a salute is being fired, crew members outside the canopy shall stand at attention facing the saluting ship. The engines are stopped, or oars laid on, at the first gun, and the boat headed up parallel to the saluting ship.

Officials or officers not having their distinctive flag or pennant flying will receive the hand salute only, whether they are in uniform or civilian clothes.

When boats with embarked officers or officials in view pass each other, hand salutes are rendered by the coxswain and senior officer embarked. The engine of the junior boat is idled during the salute. After the salute is returned, speed is resumed. Coxswains must rise while saluting and crew members outside the canopy stand at attention facing the other boat, unless it is dangerous to do so.

Salutes shall be extended to foreign military or naval officers, or officers of our own Army, Marine Corps, Naval Reserve, Naval Militia, or Coast Guard, in the same manner as to United States Navy officers of corresponding rank. This rule applies afloat and ashore.

At morning or evening colors, any boat passing near a United States Navy ship or a foreign man-of-war shall salute as follows:

Pulling boats lay on oars and powerboats stop engines. Sailing boats luff sails. Coxswains of the boats shall stand and salute, and members of a powerboat's crew outside the canopy shall stand facing toward the colors. Passengers shall sit at attention.

No junior should overhaul and pass a senior without permission. This is accomplished by the junior boat paralleling the senior boat at a respectful distance, reducing speed, and saluting. When the salute is returned, permission is considered to be granted.

Subject to the requirements of the rules for preventing collisions, junior boats must avoid crowding or embarrassing senior boats. At landings and gangways, juniors should give way to seniors. Juniors should show deference to their seniors at all times by refraining from crossing the bows of their boats or ignoring their presence.

Boats transporting seniors to a landing should be given the first opportunity to land.

Boat keepers and all other men in boats that are not under way and not carrying an officer—i.e., lying to boom or landing—shall stand and salute when an officer cruises alongside, leaves the side, or passes near them, and shall remain standing until the boat passes or reaches the ship's side. When an officer, petty officer, or acting petty officer is in charge, he alone renders the salute.

Men working on the ship's side or aboard a boat do not salute unless "Attention!" is sounded.

Coxswains in charge of boats rise and salute when officers enter or leave their boats, unless the safety of the boat would be imperiled thereby.

Boats are not to lie alongside a gangway or landing place but are to lie off while waiting. In case a long wait is probable, in bad weather or at night, permission may be asked to make fast to a boom and also for the crew to come on board.

When a visiting party goes alongside, the petty officer in charge shall go on board and obtain permission before allowing any of the visiting party to leave the boat. If permission is granted, he allows the party to come on board, each one saluting when crossing the gangway. If the boat is to wait, it shoves off and lies off the quarter, as mentioned above, unless the officer of the deck gives permission for it to haul out on the boom. The regular crew will remain in the boat unless the officer of the deck gives them permission to come on board.

Enlisted men who are passengers in the stern sheets of a boat shall always rise and salute when a commissioned officer enters or leaves the boat.

Boat Hails

Except when ship's orders are to the contrary, boats approaching the ship at night should be hailed by the quartermaster or petty officer of the watch as soon as they are close enough to hear him. The proper method of hailing the boat is to shout, "Boat ahoy!", while holding a closed fist overhead. Except when a special countersign is in use, the coxswain gives an answer to the hail that will indicate the rank of the senior person in the boat. The answers to boat hails are shown in table 11.

A powerboat approaching a ship when flag or pennant is not displayed in the boat's bow, or during the day when the curtains are so drawn that the rank of passengers cannot be distin-

Table 11. Coxswain's Boat Hail Replies

Rank or rate	Coxswain's reply
President or Vice-President of the United States	United States
Secretary of Defense, Deputy or Assistant Secretary of Defense	Defense
Secretary, Under Secretary, or Assistant Secretary of the Navy	Navy
Chief of Naval Operations, Vice Chief of Naval Operations	Naval Operations
Fleet or force commander	Fleet, or abbreviation of administrative title
General officer	General officer
Chief of staff	Staff
Flotilla commander	_____Flot_____
Squadron commander	_____Ron_____
Division commander	_____Div_____
	The type and number of abbreviation used is, for example, DesFlot-2, DesRon-6, DesDiv-22.
Marine officer commanding a brigade	Brigade commander
Commanding officer of a ship	(Name of ship)
Marine officer commanding a regiment	Regimental commander
Other commissioned officer	Aye, aye
Noncommissioned officer	No, no
Enlisted men	Hello
Boat not intending to come alongside, regardless of rank or rate of senior passenger	Passing

guished, may indicate the status of passengers by the coxswain holding up a number of fingers as shown in table 12.

Boat Gongs

A ship in port or at anchor will generally use the sounding of boat gongs to indicate the imminent departure of any one of her small craft. When used for this purpose, *three* strokes (two together plus one more) mean the boat will depart in ten minutes; two strokes mean there are five minutes to go, and one stroke means the boats will leave in one minute. This should

Table 12.   Coxswains' Hand Signals

Passenger	Number of Fingers Held Up
President of the United States	8
Secretary of the Navy	7
Assistant Secretary of the Navy	6
Admiral	6
Vice Admiral	6
Other flag officers	4
General officer	4
Commanding officer, chief of staff, or flotilla commander	3
Marine officer commanding a brigade or regiment	3
Other commissioned officers	2
All others	1

not be confused with the ceremonial sounding of boat gongs to signal the arrival or departure of some important personage.

Display of the National Ensign, Personal Flags, Pennants, and Insignia

National Ensign

The national ensign is displayed from boats of the Navy at the following times:

- When under way during daylight in a foreign port.
- When ships are required to be dressed or full dressed.
- When going alongside a foreign vessel.
- When an officer or official is embarked on an official occasion between 0800 and sunset.
- When a flag or general officer, a unit commander, a commanding officer, or a chief of staff is in uniform and is embarked in a boat of his command or in one assigned for his personal use.
- At such other times as prescribed by the senior officer present.

Because small boats are a part of a vessel, they follow the motions of the parent vessel for the half-masting of colors.

Personal Flags and Pennants

An officer in command, or a chief of staff acting for him, when embarked in a boat of a naval service on official occasions, displays from the bow of the boat his personal flag, command pennant, or if not entitled to either, his commissioning pennant.

An officer entitled to fly a personal flag or command pennant may display a miniature of such flag or pennant in the vicinity of the coxswain's station when embarked on occasions other than official in a Navy boat.

Flag Staff Insignia

The insignia on the truck of the pennant staff and flagstaff of a boat shall be as prescribed for the rank of the officer to which it belongs. The insignia on the truck of the pennant staff and flagstaff are identical and are as follows: (See figure 31 for illustrations of each.)

President	Spread eagle perched on ball
Cabinet and flag officers	Halberd head mounted on ball
Captain	Ball
Commander	Five-pointed star
Below commander	No ornaments (flat truck)

Identification Markings

Letters, numerals, and special insignia, as authorized, are fitted on both the port and the starboard bows of shipborne boats. The letters and markings must be made of chrome or brass (bright or painted) and must be of a proper level to suit the sheer of the particular type of boat. When special insignia are authorized, they must be made of sheet brass and painted as appropriate. Markings on the transoms of barges and gigs must be of gold-leaf decals.

Flag officers' barges are marked as follows:

● Chrome stars are fitted on the bow according to the arrangement on the admiral's flag.

● The official abbreviated title of the command appears on the transom in gold-leaf decal letters, i.e., SURFLANT.

SPREAD EAGLE   HALBERD   BALL

STAR   FLAT TRUCK

Figure 31. Flagstaff insignia

• Barges have black hulls. The waterline is customarily green.

Boats assigned for the personal use of *unit commanders* not of flag rank are fitted as follows:

• Broad or burgee command pennants, as appropriate, are fitted on the bow, with the squadron or division numbers superimposed, together with chrome arrows.

• The official abbreviated title of the command appears on the transom in gold-leaf decal letters, i.e., DESRON 2.

The gig for a *chief of staff* not of flag rank, is marked with the official abbreviated title of the command in chrome letters with an arrow running fore and aft through the letters. *Other boats assigned for staff use* are similarly marked except that the arrows are omitted and the letters are of brass (bright).

Boats assigned to *commanding officers of ships* are marked

on the bow with the ship type (or name) and number in chrome letters and numerals with a chrome arrow running fore and aft through the markings. The gig's waterline is, by custom, painted red. *Officers' boats* are similarly marked except that the arrow is omitted, the letters must be brass (bright), and custom dictates the use of a blue waterline. The ship's name, abbreviated name, or initials may be used in lieu of the ship's type. An assigned boat number may be used in lieu of the ship's number.

Other ship's boats are marked on the bow with either the ship's type and number followed by a dash and the boat number, such as CV 37–1, or by the ship's name, abbreviated name, or initials followed by a dash and the boat number, such as ARK–1 (for a boat belonging to the USS *Arkansas*). These markings should also appear on the transoms of all boats, except whaleboats. Letters and numbers should be of brass painted black. Type commanders have the responsibility of designating which of the above methods of marking shall be used on the boats assigned to ships under their command.

Miscellaneous small boats, such as line-handling boats, punts, and wherries, use painted numerals.

Boats and craft assigned to shore stations: District commanders may assign blocks of numbers to the individual activities within their district for permanent assignment to the boats suballotted to the various activities. The activities may assign, to each allowed boat, a consecutive number from the block provided. Each boat, except personnel boats, may then carry on each bow the abbreviation of the naval district and the consecutive number assigned. For example, Commander, Fifth Naval District might assign a block of numbers to Naval Air Station, Norfolk, which would then assign numbers to each craft allowed, such as 5ND60, 5ND61, 5ND62, and so forth. As of 1980, all but one district (Washington, D.C.) will be absorbed by a major command within each former district.

As an alternative to the foregoing, individual shore stations may use the name, or abbreviated name, of the station on each bow followed by a number commencing with 1 and running consecutively through the total number of boats assigned. Example: NS KEYWEST–1, NS KEYWEST–2, and so forth.

Personnel boats for shore-based commands normally carry on each bow the same command insignia prescribed for forces afloat. In addition, they carry the command abbreviation and location of each command neatly lettered on the transom; i.e., a COMNAV BASE, New York, barge would carry two chrome stars on each bow, and "COMNAVBASE, N.Y., N.Y." on the transom in gold-leaf decal letters. Personnel boats assigned names carry the names displayed on each bow, and the command abbreviation and geographical location of the command on the transom. Metal letters on personnel boats should be chrome-plated. Gigs carry the abbreviated name of the command in chrome letters struck through with a chrome arrow on each bow, and the location of the command on the transom in gold-leaf decals.

Amphibious forces shipborne landing craft carry black letters and numbers indicating their parent ships and craft numbers. The letters and numbers are not shaded. The following are examples of the types of abbreviations used to identify the parent ships:

Type	Abbreviation
LCC	CC
LPA	PA
LKA	KA
LHA	LHA
LSD	LSD
LST	LST
LPH	PH

Letter designations for bow ramps consist of two-letter abbreviations of the parent ships' names.

Landing craft on LSTs are similarly painted, except that LCVP ramps are marked by the ship's hull number painted black in 24-inch block numbers.

Distinguishing marks for a landing craft used as a barge, gig, or officer's boat are as described under those headings in the above paragraphs.

Combatant craft have applicable numbers painted on both bows and at the centerline of the stern. The numbers are not shaded, and the color of the numbers is such as to provide nominal contrast to the craft's color scheme.

A   Navy Boats

Dimensions, Weights, and Characteristics

Dimensions, weights, and characteristics of most standard Navy boats may be found in *Boats of the United States Navy*, NAVSEA 0283-LP-115-0000.

Table A–1 furnishes a ready reference for operating personnel of the important characteristics of most Navy boats and craft. The hoisting weights given in this table are not to be used for testing gravity davits.

Table A–1. Characteristics for Navy Boats and Craft

Boats/Craft	Length Overall	Max. Beam	HT. W.O. Cradle	Each Eng. H.P.	Fuel Cap. (Gal.)	Speed Max. Knots	No. of Crew	Hoisting[1] Weight (Lb.)	Max. Displ. (Lb.)	Cargo Cap. (Lb.)	Pers.[2] Cap.
12' Wherry (GRP)	12' 1"	4' 9"	2' 6"	15				520	1,400	880	5
14' Punt (GRP)	14' 0"	5' 2"	2' 0"				1	785	1,100	600	3
14' Wherry (Wood)	14' 1"	4' 6"	2' 6"					845	2,165	1,320	8
16' Wherry (GRP)	16' 2"	5' 10"	3' 7"					740	2,600	1,860	10
17' LHB (Wood)	17' 6"	6' 3"	4' 6"	35	6	8	2	2,900	3,560	660	4
18' TD	20' 11"	7' 4"	5' 0"	26	16	45	0	2,160	2,160		
18' TD Mk 35	20' 11"	7' 4"	3' 9"	210	42	42	1	2,830	2,830		
18' UB (GRP)	17' 6"	6' 8"	4' 0"	85	42	27	2	2,109	2,604	495	3
20' LHB (GRP)	20' 5"	7' 8"	5' 6"	50	36	10	2	4,000	4,660	660	4
22' UB	21' 10"	7' 8"	6' 0"	50	22	8	2	5,500	7,810	2,310	14
24' LSSC (GRP)	23' 2"	9' 10"	5' 6"	135	30		2	8,000	10,900	3,335	
24' PPB Mk 5	24' 9"	8' 10"	8' 2"	100	130	13	2	6,100	8,080	1,980	12
24' PPB Mk 6	24' 9"	8' 10"	8' 2"	100	60	16	2	5,900	7,880	1,980	12
26' HSL (GRP)	26' 8"	9' 8"	10' 9"	140	60	9	3	10,500	11,300	800	
26' PERS	26' 6"	9' 5"	8' 2"	230	75	21	3	9,500	11,810	2,310	14
26' PERS Mk 2	26' 6"	10' 6"	9' 4"	280	90	24	2	11,204	13,052	1,848	11
26' PERS Mk 3	26' 6"	10' 6"	8' 2"	230	85	21	2	11,394	13,242	1,848	11
26' MWB Mk 2 WD	26' 1"	7' 5"	5' 8"	25	90	7	2	6,450[3]	8,265[4]	3,300	16[5]
26' MWB Mk 5	26' 1"	8' 2"	5' 10"	25	28	7	2	6,500[3]	8,645[4]	3,300	18[5]
26' MWB Mk 6	26' 5"	8' 1"	5' 10"	25	28	7	2	6,500[3]	8,645[4]	3,300	18[5]
26' MWB Mk 7	26' 3"	8' 3"	5' 10"	25	30	7	2	6,500[3]	8,810[4]	3,300	18[5]
26' MWB Mk 8	26' 4"	7' 6"	5' 10"	25	28	7	2	6,320[3]	8,570[4]	3,100	18[5]
26' MWB Mk 9	26' 3"	8' 3"	5' 7"	25	30	7	2	6,500[3]	8,800[4]	3,300	18[5]
26' MWB Mk 10/11	26' 1"	8' 3"	6' 8"	25	30	7.5	2	6,393[3]	8,791[4]	3,223	18[5]

Designation											
28' PERS Mk 6	29' 4"	11' 0"	12' 2"	225	80	15	3	11,700	14,505	2,805	17
30' HHB	30' 6"	8' 2"	6' 10"	100	80	8	3	8,200	11,200	3,000	18
30' HHB Mk 2	30' 11"	9' 4"	7' 0"	140	80	8	3	10,193	13,381	3,198	19
31' PBR Mk 2	32' 0"	11' 8"	8' 3"	215	160		4	17,546	17,995		
33' PERS Mk 2	33' 3"	11' 4"	12' 10"	280	100	14.4	3	15,897	19,082	3,185	19
33' UB Mk 2	33' 6"	10' 10"	8' 2"	100	100	10	3	10,960	17,890	6,930	42
33' UB Mk 3	33' 10"	11' 2"	7' 3"	140	100	9.7	3	11,789	18,719	6,930	42
35' WB (Steel)	36' 1"	10' 8"	10' 1"	100	100	11	3	16,000	22,500	6,500	
35' WB (Alum.)	35' 10"	11' 2"	10' 1"	140	100	11	3	15,795	22,295	6,500	15[6]
36' ATC (Mini)	36' 0"	12' 9"	5' 11"	283	500		2	25,642	29,548	3,906	
36' HSL (GRP)	36' 0"	11' 7"	10' 8"	216	400	10	5	22,300[7]	22,000		36[6]
36' LCVP Mk 7	35' 9"	10' 7"	10' 9"	225	180	9	3	18,500	26,600	8,100	36[6]
36' LCP (L) Mk 1	36' 0"	10' 10"	7' 0"	225	180	10	3	18,500	26,600	8,100	16[8]
36' LCP (L) Mk 4	35' 10"	11' 3"	9' 11"	350	160	19	3	18,416	22,146	3,730	12[8]
36' LCP (L) Mk 11	36' 1"	13' 1"	10' 5"	270	160	17	3	17,500	20,200	2,700	26
36' UB MSSC	36' 0"	12' 0"	8' 0"	325	300		4	19,779	24,227	4,448	
39' ASB (GRP)	39' 0"	11' 3"	13' 6"	216	400	10.3	6	24,300[7]	24,000		8
40' AVR Mk 2	44' 3"	12' 5"	12' 6"	450	200	21	5	25,900	27,220	1,320	40
40' PERS Mk 1/2	40' 2"	11' 7"	15' 9"	165	165	12	3	16,500	23,100	6,600	39
40' PERS Mk 4	40' 3"	12' 1"	12' 8"	280	105	15.9	3	19,280	25,765	6,485	38
40' PERS Mk 5	41' 7"	11' 10"	13' 5"	280	180	19.7	3	22,500	28,800	6,300	11
40' PPRB Mk 3	41' 4"	11' 9"	12' 10"	280	380	20	4	26,000	30,100	4,100	71
40' UB (Wood)	40' 2"	12' 2"	8' 6"	165	120	11	4	17,600	29,315	11,715	71
40' UB Mk 2	40' 1"	12' 2"	9' 4"	165	120	11	4	16,000	27,715	11,715	70
40' UB Mk 3/4	40' 1"	12' 2"	9' 4"	165	112	10.3	4	16,835	28,445	11,610	12
45' AVR	45' 9"	13' 9"	16' 6"	630	375	33	6	32,000	34,000	2,000	
45' Picket Mk 1, 2, 3	45' 9"	13' 9"	12' 6"	380	375	20	5	32,000	35,850	3,850	
45' Picket Mk 5	46' 4"	15' 3"	12' 6"	450	375	13	5	33,200	39,320	6,120	
45' UB (Steel)	45' 6"	12' 10"	20' 0"	300	340		3	31,300	33,800	2,500	
50' PCF Mk 1	50' 2"	13' 1"	17' 6"	430	800	16.2	6	43,000	42,500		15

Table A-1. Characteristics for Navy Boats and Craft (Cont.)

Boats/Craft	Length Overall	Max. Beam	HT. W.O. Cradle	Each Eng. H.P.	Fuel Cap. (Gal.)	Speed Max. Knots	No. of Crew	Hoisting[1] Weight (Lb.)	Max. Displ. (Lb.)	Cargo Cap. (Lb.)	Pers.[2] Cap.
50' PCF Mk 2	51' 4"	13' 7"	17' 6"	430	828		6	43,035	43,035		
50' PCF Mk 3	51' 5"	14' 11"	15' 10"	425	828		6	44,848	49,019		
50' ASPB	50' 2"	15' 3"	16' 6"	430	620	11	5	53,815	58,500		
50' UB (Wood)	50' 3"	14' 6"	10' 6"	165	170	9.8	4	23,330	47,390	4,685	145
50' UB Mk 4	50' 3"	14' 11"	10' 6"	165	170	16	4	26,338	50,088	24,060	142
50' ACC	51' 1"	15' 1"	17' 0"	330	360		4		34,200	33,750	
50' LCM (3)	50' 2"	14' 1"	16' 3"	225	450	9.5	5	52,075	112,075	60,000	
50' MDT	50' 7"	14' 6"	17' 0"	165	400	10	5	43,200[8]	47,575	4,375	
52' LCSR	52' 5"	14' 10"	17' 0"	1,000	1,300		4	47,000	50,000	3,000	18
52' Sounding	52' 2"	14' 7"	18' 3"	165	1,470	10	10	67,200	73,648	6,448	
54' TD Mk 35	54' 9"	13' 8"	16' 2"	325	550	35	4	36,068	39,375		
56' LCM (6) MOD 1	56' 2"	14' 1"	17' 2"	225	450	9	5	56,000	124,000	68,000	120
56' LCM (6) MOD 2	56' 0"	14' 4"	13' 5"	165	490	10.2	5	56,163	127,730	68,000	120
63' AVR Mk 3-4	63' 4"	15' 4"	15' 6"	630	1,580	28	8	62,800[9]	64,600	1,800	
65' ASRB (Alum.)	65' 0"	17' 3"	17' 6"	585	800	24	6	70,800	69,400		10
65' PB Mk 3	64' 11"	18' 1"	18' 7"	650	1,800		5	83,000	82,500		
65' TRB (Alum.)	65' 0"	17' 3"	19' 6"	504	800	18.7	6	78,456	79,350	11,100	
72' TRB Mk 2	72' 9"	17' 0"	20' 0"	500	1,800	18	6	92,300	116,300	24,000	
73' NMB	73' 5"	17' 1"	20' 3"	650	1,200	17	7		111,840		
74' LCM (8) Steel	73' 7"	21' 1"	15' 7"	510	875	9	5	131,326	260,567	120,000	
74' LCM (8) Alum.	74' 6"	21' 1"	15' 7"	510	875	12	5	83,562	213,562	130,000	
85' PB (2 Screw)	85' 0"	18' 8"	17' 0"	700	2,850	21.7	8	100,000	120,000		
85' PB (3 Screw)	85' 0"	18' 8"	17' 0"	620	3,850	23.7	8	102,000	133,600		
100' TWR (Steel)[10]	102' 0"	21' 0"	28' 6"	800	8,695	18	15		368,995	38,500	

135' LCU (1637CL)	134' 9"	29' 9"	16' 1"	600	7,004	12	6	799,680	320,320
135' LCU (1646CL)	134' 9"	29' 9"	16' 1"	600	3,380	11	6	873,600	320,320

[1] The hoisting weight of a boat is defined as the weight of the boat completely fitted out and ready for service with machinery and electrical installations in operating condition. All outfit, on board repair parts, navigational and lifesaving equipment, or their equivalent weights, must be on board. Weights representing the crew at 165 pounds per man must also be on board; fuel tanks must be full except for special cases.

[2] Personnel capacity shown is exclusive of crew. See BOATALT 26' MWB/10A for Restrictive Limits of Personnel Capacities for Forward Compartments all 26' MWB's.

[3] Lifesaving crew of five plus two rescued, total seven persons.

[4] Open condition, only NAVSEA approved canopies shall be installed.

[5] Capacities for forward compartment of MWB's Mark 5, 6, 7, 9, and 10 are 11 men.

[6] The weight of a marine, ready for combat, is 225 pounds. These craft are hoisted at the davits in a fully loaded condition; at the slings in hoisting condition. All weights are approximate only and should not be used for design purposes.

[7] Hoisted in fully-loaded condition.

[8] Light ship condition.

[9] Hoisted with cradle.

[10] Weight data taken from Inclining Experiment Report; no Scale Weight Reports available.

36' LCP (L) Mk 4[10]

100' TWR (Steel)[10]

Table A–2. Characteristics for Inflatable Lifeboats

Boat Type	Capacity	Wgt (lbs)[1]	Dimensions Inflated		Dimensions—Case/Container		
			L	W	H	W	L
Mk 2	7 persons	190	12'0"	5'9"	24"	18"	50"
					Fabric Container		
Mk 5 Mod 1	15 persons	380	15'8"	7'4"	30"	26"	60"
					Fabric Container		
Mk 5 Mod 2	15 persons	450	15'8"	7'4"	27"	dia	56"
					Rigid Container		
Mk 6	25 persons	515	17'9¾"	8'10½"	27"	dia	56"
					Rigid Container		

[1] Boat packed in carrying case complete with water, rations, and survival gear.

Illustrations of Some Common Navy Boats

26' Motor Whaleboat, MK 9

Purpose: Lifeboat, officer's boat, gigs, shore-party boat, mail boat
Capacity: 20 men including crew
Crew: 2 men
Length, overall: 26'2⅞"
Beam: 8'2⅜" maximum
Draft: 2'7" loaded
Full load displacement: 8,800 lbs
Hoisting weight: 5,600 lbs, 6,500 lbs outfitted as lifeboat
Hoisted by: Slings or davits
Construction: Round bottom, single skin fiberglass reinforced plastic
Speed: 7 knots at full load displacement
Fuel capacity: 30 gallons
Range: 110 nautical miles at full power and full load
NavShips Drawing No.: MTRWHAL26MK9-145-1847404
Stock No.: 1940-678-0943 (open)
          1940-680-4653 (canopied)

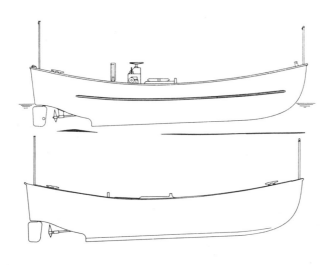

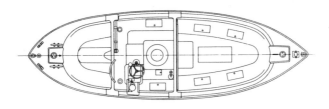

Engine details: 1 Gray marine model 4D-129, 25 hp @ 2,000
    rpm, hull cooled, 24-v DC electric system
Federal Stock No.: S2815-516-7451
Propeller: 18″ by 14″ P by 1⅜″ bore rh rotation

28′ Personnel Boat, MK 2

Purpose: To transport personnel
Capacity: 22 men including crew
Crew: 2 men
Length overall: 29′2⅝″
Beam: 10′11¾″ maximum

Draft: 2′9″ loaded
Full load displacement: 12,600 lbs
Hoisting weight: 9,300 lbs
Hoisted by: Sling or davits
Construction: V-bottom, wood frame, plywood planked
Speed: 16 knots at full load displacement
Fuel capacity: 90 gallons
Range: 120 nautical miles at full power and full load
NavShips Drawing No.: S8227(1)–28–753080
Stock No.: S1940–268–9995
Engine details: (*a*) 1 6-cylinder diesel, 165 hp at 1,800 rpm. Detroit diesel engine division, model 64HN10, hull cooled, 24-volt electrical system. Stock No. S75–E–53737–4176
or:(*b*) 1 6-cylinder diesel, 165 hp at 1,800 rpm (continuous), 225 hp at 2,100 rpm (emergency). Detroit diesel engine division, model 64HN10, inboard heat exchanger, 12-volt electrical system. Stock No. S75–E–53737–4160
Propeller details: 1 20″ D by 16″ P by 1¾″ bore, lh rotation. Stock No. HM60MWL–30097

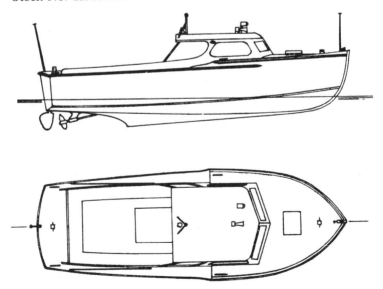

36' Landing Craft-LCVP (Wood)

Purpose: To land and retrieve personnel or equipment during amphibious operations

Capacity: 39 men including crew or 8,595 lbs including passengers and crew

Crew: 3 men

Length overall: 35'9"

Beam: 10'6¼" maximum

Draft: 3'5" loaded

Full load displacement: 26,600 lbs

Hoisting weight: 18,500 lbs

Hoisted by: Sling or davit

Construction: V-bottom, wood frame, plywood sides with ¼" sts armor, double-planked bottom (plywood inner, carvel outer)

Speed: 9 knots at full load displacement

Fuel capacity: 180 gallons

Range: 110 nautical miles at full power and full load

NavShips Drawing No.: LCVP–8510, LCVP–8860 (keel cooled)

Stock Nos.: S1905–153–6697 (12-volt)

S1905–294–2215 (keel cooled)

Engine details: (a) 1 6-cylinder diesel, 225 hp at 2,100 rpm (emergency), 165 hp at 1,800 rpm (continuous), Gray marine model 64HN9, inboard heat exchanger, 12-volt electrical system. Stock No. S75–E–53737–8240

or: (b) 1 6-cylinder diesel 225 hp at 2,100 rpm (emergency), 165 hp at 1,800 rpm (continuous), Gray marine model 64HN9, hull cooled, 12-volt electrical system. Stock No. S75–E–53737–8244

or: (c) 1 6-cylinder diesel, 225 hp at 2,100 rpm (emergency), 165 hp at 1,800 rpm (continuous), Gray marine model 64HN9, hull cooled, 24-volt electrical system. Stock No. S75–E–53737–8241

Propeller details: 1 22" D by 20" P by 2" bore, rh rotation, Stock No. HF60MWL–30014

Cargo well: Approximate dimensions: 18'3" long, 6'4½" wide, 4'8" deep

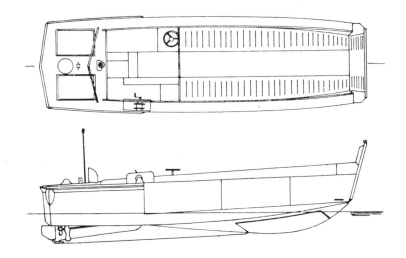

40′ Utility Boat, MK 2

Purpose: To transport personnel or cargo
Capacity: 75 men including crew
Crew: 4 men
Length overall: 40′1″
Beam: 12′2″ maximum
Draft: 2′8¼″ loaded
Full load displacement: 27,715 lbs
Hoisting weight: 16,000 lbs
Hoisted by: Slings and davits
Construction: Fiberglass reinforced plastic, round bottom
Speed: 11 knots at full load displacement
Fuel capacity: 120 gallons
Range: 110 nautical miles at full power and full load
NavShips Drawing No.: S8228(4)–40–1428868
Stock No.: S1940–529–9725
Engine details: Diesel, 64HN9, 2 cycle, 6 cylinder, 165 hp at
  1,800 rpm, hull cooled, 24-volt electrical system. Stock No.
  S2815–132–8621
Propeller details: 1 26″ D by 17″ P by 2″ bore, rh rotation

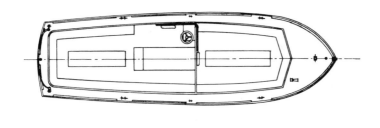

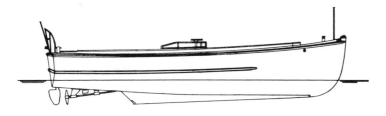

40′ Personnel Boat, MK 5

Purpose: To transport officer personnel and for conversion to gigs and barges

Capacity: 43 men including crew

Crew: 3 men

Length overall: 41′6¼″

Beam: 11′9¼″ maximum

Draft: 3′10″ loaded

Full load displacement: 28,800 lbs

Hoisting wgt: 22,500 lbs

Hoisted by: Slings

Construction: Round bottom, single skin, fiberglass reinforced plastic

Speed: 18 knots at full load displacement

Fuel capacity: 180 gallons

Range: 100 nautical miles at full power and full load

NavShips Drawing No.: PERS40MK5–145–2089681

Stock No.: 1940–072–5712

Engine details: 2 diesel, Detroit engines, 6087N, 250 hp @ 1,550 rpm, 12-volt electrical system

Fed. Stock No.: S1940–072–5712
Propeller: 2 26″ D by 18″ P × 2″ bore, 1 rh rotation, 1 lh rotation

50′ Motor Launch

Purpose: To transport personnel or cargo
Capacity: 150 men including crew
Crew: 4 men
Length overall: 50′2″
Beam: 13′2″ maximum
Draft: 4′3½″ loaded
Full load displacement: 47,390 lbs
Hoisting weight: 23,300 lbs
Hoisted by: Sling
Construction: Round bottom, wood frame, carvel planked
Speed: 8 knots at full load displacement
Fuel capacity: 80 gallons
Range: 150 nautical miles at full power and full load
NavShips Drawing No.: 142681
Stock No.: S1940–268–9993
Engine details: 1 6-cylinder diesel, 60 hp at 1,700 rpm. Navy type DB, Navy design cylinder head, direct water cooled, 24-volt electrical system. Stock No. S75–E–53744–6226
Propeller details: 1 24″ D by 26″ P by 1¾″ bore, rh rotation. Stock No. GF60–P–9048

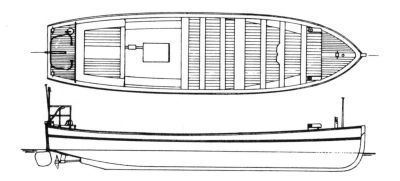

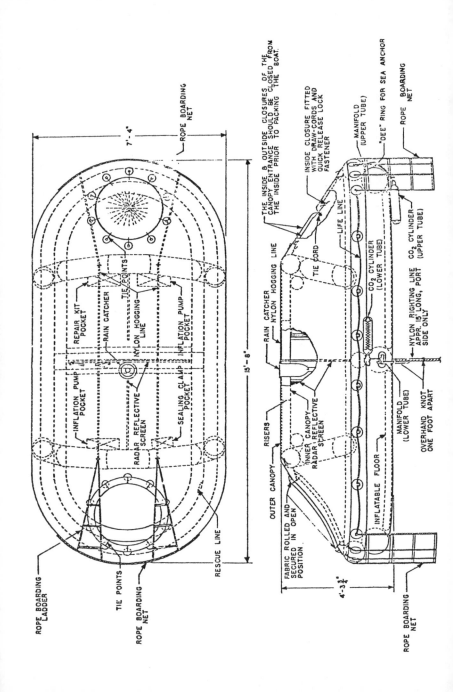

B Checklists

Daily Boat Inspection Checklist

- Engine (test)
- Hull (intact, plugs present)
- Lights (test)
  Port (red)
  Stbd (green)
  Stern (white)
  Bow (on mast, white)
- Horn (test)
- Bell
- Life rings (2)
- Life jackets (Inherently buoyant. Number aboard equal to boat's max. capacity.)
- Compass (mounted and lighted)
- Portable (removable) hull parts
- Emergency tiller
- Boat hook
- Anchor
- Anchor rope
- Ensign (as needed)
- Flag staff
- Fire extinguisher (with up-to-date tag)
- First aid kit
- Boat log
- Recall and lifeboat signals (posted)
- Max. operating speed (posted)
- Fueling instructions (posted)
- Standing order to coxswains
- Harbor charts (as needed)

Boat Officer/Coxswain/Boat Engineer Pre-Underway Check-Off List

The following is a sample pre-underway check-off list for ships' boats. This guide, furnished by the USS *Lawrence*, DDG–4, may be used by individual units to construct an applicable check-off list for their own ship's boats.

Before Boat is Lowered into the Water

Initials

_____ 1) Check bilge plugs to ensure they are in.

_____ 2) Inspect screw and propeller and ensure they are not loose.

_____ 3) Inspect rubber exhaust boots, overboard discharge, and intake lines.

_____ 4) Inspect sea strainers.

_____ 5) Check engine's lube, transmission, and fuel oil levels.

_____ 6) Check freshwater level in expansion tank.

_____ 7) Inspect all lines and fittings on engine, transmission, and pumps.

_____ 8) Ensure foot valve for bilge pump is unobstructed.

_____ 9) Ensure blower flaps door is opened and locked.

_____10) Inspect belt tension.

_____11) Inspect bilge/engine compartment for loose tools, equipment, or rags.

_____12) Ensure tools are on board.

After Boat Is in the Water

_____ 1) Inspect shaft and rudder post packing glands for leaks.

_____ 2) Inspect bilge plugs, exhaust boots, and engine compartments for leaks.

_____ 3) Start engine and inspect overboard discharges to ensure proper operation of the cooling system.

_____ 4) Check all gauges for proper operation.

Before Each Run

_____ 1) Check oil and fuel level.

_____ 2) Check expansion tank level.
_____ 3) Check belt tensions.
_____ 4) Check to ensure that the blower flapper door is opened and locked.
_____ 5) Check sea strainers.
_____ 6) Check engine compartment for oil, fuel, and/or water leaks.

After Engine Is Started (Each time)

_____ 1) Check for cooling water discharge and exhaust.
_____ 2) Check temperatures and pressure gauges.
_____ 3) Inspect engine compartments for water, oil, fuel and/or water leaks.

"Ready for Lowering" Checklist

A power lifeboat is "ready for lowering" when:

• The crew of the watch has been mustered, each man is at his station in the boat or at the falls, winch, or crane, and each man understands his duties at man overboard; this includes the men for handling the winch, steadying lines, tripping line, sea painter, and for signaling.

• The boat is located in an outboard stowage position on radial, crescent, triple, or quadruple-banked gravity-type davits and griped down securely with gripes fitted with quick-releasing pelican hooks or toggles.

• Power is on the crane or winch, with tension on wire rope falls, or if the davits are equipped with manila rope falls, the rope falls are rove at the davit heads and the automatic releasing hooks fitted. At night, the manila falls are coiled down on deck or in racks and clear for running; during the day the coils may be triced up the davits with becket and toggle. (Wire rope falls are always attached to the winch drum.)

• The boat is stowed under a crane; the sling ring is hooked on the single whip of the crane; and the tripping line, used to release the sling ring from the hook on the crane, is rove off, clear, and coiled down ready for paying out.

- Forward and after steadying lines are rigged and coiled down ready for paying out when the boat is hoisted out and lowered.
- The sea painter is secured a little abaft the bow of the boat on the inboard side and led clear.
- The fuel tanks are full.
- The lubricating oil reservoir is full and a reserve can of lubricating oil is in the boat.
- The required fire extinguishers are in the boat.
- Life preservers, one for each member of the crew, are stowed in a locker adjacent to the lifeboat so that the crew can don them before manning the boat. If this is not practicable, life jackets must be secured in place, one under each position occupied in the boat when the boat is lowered.
- The bilges are dry.
- The boat plugs are in place.
- A suitable light for blinker signaling is in place.
- All articles of the boat equipment are ready for use.
- Two days supply of water and provisions for the crew are in place.
- Lifelines or manropes are available for all personnel manning the boat.

C Special Equipment

Equipment Listing for Aircraft Rescue Kit

- Bridge equipment

  One   Portable electric megaphone.

- Swimmers' equipment (for either ship or boat recovery)

  Two   Skin divers' wet suits, including hood, gloves, and boots

  Two   Skin divers' masks

  Two (pairs)   Skin divers' fins

  Two   Belt harnesses

  Two   Tending lines—nylon 800-pound test, 300 yards in length

- MWB or rescue boat equipment (boat recovery)

  One   Boat hook

  Two   Grappling hooks

  One   Knife (sharp)

  One   Shears, material cutting, hand, stock GM5110–242–2861

  One   Rescue knife, FSN 9G1–5510–524–6924

  One   Spare blade, FSN 9G1–5510–098–4325

  One   Shroud cutter

  One   Hatchet or axe

  Two   Lanterns

  Five   Flashlights

  One   Radio set, portable

  One   Semaphore flags set

  One   Hand-held signal flasher

  One   First aid kit

Table C–1.   Boat Rescue Equipment

Quantity	Description
1	Boat hook
2	Grappling hooks (7 lb, 100 feet, ¾-inch circumferènce nylon line spliced to chain)
1	Shears, material-cutting, hand
1	Rescue knife (MC–1)
1	Hatchet or axe
2	Battle lanterns
5	Flashlights
1	Radio set, portable (PRC–90*) and (Motorola HT 220)
1 (set)	Semaphore flags
1	Hand-held signal light
1	First aid kit with air way
1	Boarding ladder
2	Sav-a-Life ball
1	Sling, survivor rescue
1	Very pistol with red-white-green flares
1	M-14 rifle and bandolier of ammunition
2	Blankets
1	Swimmer/survivor tending line, yellow polypropylene 800-pound test, 300 yards long, equipped with a compact reel and a quick-release hook fitted on the end for attaching to swimmer/survivor harness "D" ring.

* Required for each swimmer.

Table C–2.   Mark 5 (15-person capacity) and Mark 6 (26-person capacity) Inflatable Lifeboats

Item	Quantity
Survival Gear[1]	
Bailer, plastic, 2-quart capacity	1
Battery, dry, flashlight, alkaline (Size D)[2]	4
Desalter kits, Type II	5
Fishing kit, survival	1
Flashlight, Type II, Style 1	1
Flashlight bulbs (PR 6)	1
Food packets	75 (Mk 5)
	125 (Mk 6)
Kit, first aid	1
Kit, signaling	1 carton of
	12 units
Knife, pocket	1
Measuring cup, plastic, 8 ounce	2
Mirror, signaling emergency, Type II	1
Motion sickness tablets, dimenhydrinate, 50 milligram	200 (Mk 5)
Openers, beer-can type	4 (Mk 5)
	6 (Mk 6)
Sea marker, fluorescein, canister type	1
Sponge, cellulose, Type 1, Size 10	2
Storage bag, drinking water, Size A	2
Water, canned, 10-ounce cans	50 (Mk 5)
	75 (Mk 6)
Whistle, signaling, plastic Type II	1
Equipment to be Stowed with Each Lifeboat	
Floatable knife	1
Hand pumps	2
Oars	4
Operation and Maintenance Manual	2
Rescue line	1
Pliers, pair	1
Scissors	1
Sea Anchor and line	2
Sealing clamp, 3 inches	2
Sealing clamp, 5 inches	2
Sealing clamp, 7½ inches	2
Survival gear bag	1
Valve adapter	2

[1] Inflatable lifeboats in rigid containers will have the survival gear packed in a watertight survival gear bag prior to installation aboard ship. Inflatable lifeboats in fabric containers will have the survival gear packed in watertight bags that are stowed in the appropriate pockets of the lifeboat container.

[2] Standard D-cell flashlight batteries may be retained if the date stamped on the bottom does not indicate age in excess of one year (that is, 0274 indicates month (February) and year (1974)).

Table C–3. Abandon Ship Boats

Item	Quantity
Survival Gear[1,2]	
Bailer, plastic, 2-quart capacity	1
Battery, dry, flashlight, alkaline (Size D)[3]	4
Desalter kits, Type II	5
Fishing kit, survival	1
Flashlight, Type II, Style I	1
Flashlight bulbs	1
Food packets	125
Kit, first aid	1
Kit, signaling	1 carton of 12 units
Knife, pocket	1
Measuring cup, plastic, 8 ounce	2
Mirror, signaling emergency, Type II	2
Motion sickness tablets, dimenhydrinate, 50 milligram	250
Openers, beer-can type	6
Painter, 2-inch circ. manila or nylon, length 40 yards	2
Pliers, pair	1
Sea marker, fluorescein, canister type	1
Shark repellent containers	2
Sponge, cellulose, Type 1, Size 10	2
Storage bag, drinking water, Size A	2
Water, canned, 10-ounce cans	75
Whistle, signaling, plastic Type II	1
Equipment to be Stowed with Each Abandon Ship Boat	
Paddles	4
Boat cover (Rescue Orange) with rigging (for boats not having a fixed canopy)	1
Information to be provided by NAVSHIPS 429	
Scissors	1

[1] Survival gear carried by abandon ship boats shall be stowed in a watertight survival gear bag and placed in a weathertight box. The box and paddles and boat cover shall be placed on a bulkhead or deck adjacent to the boat. A plastic label plate with the legend "ABANDON SHIP EQUIPMENT—LOAD INTO BOAT UPON ABANDON SHIP SIGNAL" shall be posted on the box.

[2] Items of equippage designated herein shall be packaged in accordance with NAVSHIPS Publication N.S. 0902–137–7010.

[3] Standard D-cell flashlight batteries may be retained if the date stamped on the bottom does not indicate age in excess of one year (that is, 0274 indicates month (February) and year (1974)).

D   Special Signals

Boat Call Signals

Occasionally it is necessary to call personnel and boats by means of a flaghoist. The PAPA flag is the general recall when shown in port. It is flown from the foretruck, or where seen best, and means: All personnel belonging to this ship return immediately.

QUEBEC, while flying, means: All boats belonging to this ship (or boats addressed) return to the ship immediately.

If for any reason it is desired to call a particular boat, a hoist is flown as follows: QUEBEC, followed by a *numeral pennant*, which designates a type of boat, and one or more additional *numeral flags* to indicate the number of the boat.

The calls for the various types of boats follow.

Qp0	All boats.
Qp1	Admiral's barge.
Qp2	Chief of staff barge or gig.
Qp3	Staff gigs or motorboats.
Qp4	Captain's gig.
Qp5	Boats under power.
Qp6	Boats under sail.
Qp7	Boats under oars.
Qp8	Reserved for local assignment by COs;
to	
Qp5p0	Calls usually are assigned according to boat numbers.

An example of a call to own ship's boat is Qp52 (that is pennant 5, flag 2) meaning own ship's powerboat number 2.

To call another ship's boat, the ship's call is placed under the boat call. For example, Qp4Rp1p4 calls the captain's gig of carrier 14.

Table D–1. Rescue-Boat Signals from Ship to Boat and from Boat to Ship

From Ship to Boat

Flag or Blinker	Pyrotechnics	Meaning
Three	One white star	Steer straight away from ship.
Three Port	One red star	Steer left (or to port). When hauled down, cease turn and steady on present course.
Three Stbd	One green star	Steer right (or to starboard). When hauled down, cease turn and steady on present course.
Eight	Two green stars	Steer straight toward ship.
Quebec	Two red stars	Return to ship.

From Boat to Ship

Visual Signals	Pyrotechnics	Meaning
Blinker or semaphore, plain language	One green star	Cannot find man.
	One white star	Have recovered man.
	One red star	Need assistance.

Engine Signals

In larger boats, the coxswain will not have direct manual control of the engine(s) but will transmit engine orders to the boat engineer for execution. A system of bell signals has been devised (for use in such cases) as follows:

• To get the engine started, the coxswain strikes the bell twice. Two strokes mean: "Engine running, clutch disengaged." If the engine is already running with clutch engaged, two strokes mean: "Throw out the clutch."

• He strikes the bell once for "Ahead slow." If already running at full speed, one stroke on the bell means: "Reduce speed to ahead slow."

• Four strokes on the bell mean: "Full speed in direction propeller is turning when signal is given."

• Three strokes mean: "Back slow speed." Signals are always given in order, and no required signal may be left out. That is, a boat sounds one stroke to slow the engine when going ahead full; two, to disengage the clutch; and three to back slow, before sounding four to back full.

Somewhere in the boat there usually is a metal plate on which the bell signals to the engineer are tabulated as follows:

Number	Meaning
1 bell	Ahead slow.
2 bells	Engine idling, clutch out.
3 bells	Back slow.
4 bells	Full speed in direction propeller is turning when signal is given.

Distress and Emergency Signals (Excerpt from the *National Search and Rescue Manual*, NWP–37)

The following are recognized distress signals under the International Rules of the Road (Annex IV) and are customarily accepted under the Inland Rules, although only signals (b) and (h) are specifically mentioned.

1. (a) A gun or other explosive signal fired at intervals of about a minute.
   (b) A continuous sounding with any fog-signaling apparatus.
   (c) Rockets or shells, throwing red stars fired one at a time at short intervals.
   (d) A signal made by radiotelegraphy or by any other signaling method consisting of the group SOS in the Morse code.
   (e) A signal sent by radiotelephony consisting of the spoken word "Mayday."
   (f) The International Code Signal of distress indicated by the code group NC. (See the International Code of Signals—H.O. 102 for other code groups with emergency significance.)
   (g) A signal consisting of a square flag having above or below it a ball or anything resembling a ball.
   (h) Flames on the vessel (as from a burning tar barrel, oil barrel, etc.).
   (i) A rocket parachute flare or a hand flare showing a red light.

(j) A smoke signal giving off a volume of orange-colored smoke.

(k) Slowly and repeatedly raising and lowering arms outstretched to each side.

(l) The radiotelegraph alarm signal (which is designed to actuate the radiotelegraph auto alarms of vessels so fitted, consisting of a series of 12 dashes, sent in 1 minute, the duration of each dash being 4 seconds, and the duration of the interval between 2 consecutive dashes being 1 second).

(m) The radiotelephone alarm signal (consisting of 2 tones transmitted alternately over periods of from 30 seconds to 1 minute).

These signals may be supplemented with signals from HO–102, the *International Code of Signals*, of which an excerpt follows below.

Selected Single-Letter Signals (Excerpt from H.O. 102)

The following messages may be made by any method of signaling.

A I have a diver down; keep well clear at slow speed.

*B I am taking in, discharging, or carrying dangerous goods.

C Affirmative, or The significance of the previous group should be read in the affirmative.

*D Keep clear of me; I am maneuvering with difficulty.

*E I am altering my course to starboard.

F I am disabled; communicate with me.

G I require a pilot. (When made by fishing vessels operating in close proximity on the fishing grounds it means: I am hauling nets.

*H I have a pilot on board.

*I I am altering my course to port.

**K I wish to communicate with you.

L You should stop your vessel instantly.

M My vessel is stopped and making no way through the water.

N Negative, or The significance of the previous group should be read in the negative.

O Man overboard.

P In harbor—All persons should report on board as the vessel is about to proceed to sea.

**S My engines are going astern.

*T Keep clear of me; I am engaged in pair trawling.

U You are running into danger.

V I require assistance.

W I require medical assistance.

X Stop carrying out your intentions and watch for my signals.

Y I am dragging my anchor.

Note: When these or any other signals from H.O. 102 are sent between two U.S. Navy vessels, they must be proceeded by the "Code or Answer" pennant.

*Signals of letters marked by an asterisk (*) when made by sound may only be made in compliance with the requirements of the International Regulations for Preventing Collisions at Sea (Rules 15 and 28).
**Special meanings as landing signals for small boats with crews or persons in distress. (International Convention on the Safety of Life at Sea, 1960, Chapter 5, Regulation 16.)

NUMERAL PENNANTS

PENNANT and NAME	Spoken	Written		PENNANT FOUR	p4		PENNANT EIGHT	p8
1	PENNANT ONE	p1	5	PENNANT FIVE	p5	9	PENNANT NINE	p9
2	PENNANT TWO	p2	6	PENNANT SIX	p6	Ø	PENNANT ZERO	pØ
3	PENNANT THREE	p3	7	PENNANT SEVEN	p7			

ALPHABETIC AND NUMERAL FLAGS

FLAG and NAME	Spoken	Written	FLAG and NAME	Spoken	Written	FLAG and NAME	Spoken	Written
A	ALFA	A	M	MIKE	M	Y	YANKEE	Y
B	BRAVO	B	N	NOVEMBER	N	Z	ZULU	Z
C	CHARLIE	C	O	OSCAR	O	1	ONE	1
D	DELTA	D	P	PAPA	P	2	TWO	2
E	ECHO	E	Q	QUEBEC	Q	3	THREE	3
F	FOXTROT	F	R	ROMEO	R	4	FOUR	4
G	GOLF	G	S	SIERRA	S	5	FIVE	5
H	HOTEL	H	T	TANGO	T	6	SIX	6
I	INDIA	I	U	UNIFORM	U	7	SEVEN	7
J	JULIETT	J	V	VICTOR	V	8	EIGHT	8
K	KILO	K	W	WHISKEY	W	9	NINE	9
L	LIMA	L	X	XRAY	X	Ø	ZERO	Ø

E Boat Officer PQS Theory

This section directs your attention to the terms, principles, and laws of Boat Officer Theory, as defined by the Navy Personnel Qualifications Standard System.

Definitions

Define the following items:
  Harbor charts
  Boat gongs
  Tiller
  Bowhook
  Fenders
  Flagstaff insignia
  Boat log
  Barge
  Gig
  Motor whaleboat
  Utility boat
  Personnel boat
  Personal flag/broad and burgee command pennants

Boat Security

State when a boat officer should be assigned.

State what equipment should be carried on board a boat to ensure safe navigation.

State the requirements for life preservers.

State the required signaling equipment.

Discuss fire hazards in powerboats.

Boat Operations

Discuss the responsibilities and authority of the coxswain.

Discuss the responsibilities and authority of the boat officer.

Describe the relationship between the boat officer and an embarked line or staff officer who is senior.

Describe the duties of the engineman and bowhook.

Explain the proper technique for loading a large liberty boat.

Discuss the effect of reduced visibility on boat operations.

Discuss the following with respect to ship's boat loading:

Loading—normal conditions

Loading—heavy-weather conditions

Location of boat manning placard

Discuss boat gongs and their meaning.

Discuss the proper procedures for shoving off a boat and the commands issued.

Boat Honors and Ceremonies

Discuss honors and ceremonies rendered between boats, including the duties of the boat officer.

Discuss the use and meaning of boat hails between the quarterdeck and approaching boats.

Discuss the bow and flagstaff insignia for boats.

Discuss the use of personal flags and pennants and the broad and burgee command pennant on boats.

Discuss the painting of boats and the significance of the colors used.

F   Boating Terms and Definitions

Boat crews should be able to identify each part or piece of their boat by its proper name and also know the meaning of all phrases and terms pertaining to boats and their handling. The following list of definitions is of particular interest to boat crewmen[1]:

Abaft. Toward the stern of a ship; back; behind; back of; farther aft than.

Abeam. Alongside at right angles to the keel.

Abreast. Side by side; over against; opposite to.

Accommodation Ladder. A flight of steps leading down a ship's side by which small boats may be entered or the ship boarded. Often erroneously called a gangway.

Adrift. Without being fast to a stationary object.

Avast. Order to stop or cease.

Awash. The condition when the seas break over a wreck or shoal, or when a vessel is so low that water is constantly washing aboard in quantities.

Back Wash. The water thrust aft by the action of the screw.

Bank. A large navigable shoal with a sufficient depth of water to prevent the sea breaking. Dangerous reefs and shoals may exist on banks.

Bar. A shoal usually of sand or mud opposite a river mouth or harbor entrance.

[1](Condensed from the USS *Iwo Jima Handbook for Boat Crewmen*, and from *Nomenclature of Naval Vessels*, NAVSEA 0900–LP–029–7010)

Barge. A general name given to a large pulling boat. It is often given to flat-bottomed craft, but more particularly to vessels built for towage purposes. Formerly the term was applied to the elegantly fitted boats of vessels of state, and we still have the admiral's barge, which is a boat for this officer's use.

Beacon. An aid to navigation, usually unlighted. Beacons take various forms to be conspicuous and characteristic, and often carry cages, balls, diamonds, cones, etc., as topmarks.

Beam. The extreme width of a vessel.

Bell Buoy. A floating (usually unlighted) beacon equipped with a bell so installed as to ring automatically.

Belly Band, Strap. A rope around a small boat from which a kedge anchor is suspended.

Bending Shackle. Connects the chain to the anchor. It is heavier than the shackles between the different shots of chain.

Bilge. The turn of the hull below the waterline; that part of the inside hull above the keelson where bilge water collects.

Binnacle. A stand or case for housing a compass so that it may be conveniently read.

Bitts. A pair of short steel posts or horns on board ship used to secure lines. *See* Cleat, Bollard.

Boat Boom A spar swung out horizontally and at right angles from the side of a vessel, supported by topping lift and guys. A small boat rides to it without fouling the ship.

Boat Engineer. Enlisted crew member in charge of maintaining boat engines.

Boat Chocks Cradles in which a boat rests on the deck of a vessel.

Boat Fall. The rope and blocks that make up a tackle with which to raise and lower boats. The fall has a hauling part and a standing part, the latter being the end fast to the tail of the block. With some, only the hauling part is the fall.

Boat Gripe. Device for securing a boat at its davits or in its cradle.

Boat Hook. A longhandled device for catching hold of a ring bolt or frap line when coming alongside a vessel or pier in a small boat.

Bollard. Steel or iron post on a pier or wharf, used in securing a ship's mooring lines.

Breakwater. An artificial embankment to break the force of the seas and furnish shelter behind it. A low bulkhead on the forward deck to take the force of a boarding sea and protect the hatches.

Brow. A portable ramp between the ship and a pier or wharf. A gangplank.

Bum Boat. A small craft used to bring out peddlers who supply the crew with fruit, tobacco, parrots, canes, and perhaps illicit wants.

Buoys. Floating aids to navigation, which by their shape and color convey to the mariner valuable information as to his position.

Call Away (Whaleboat). A preliminary order given when a boat is to leave the ship. Away (Whaleboat) is the order given by the boatswain.

Camel. A floating stage very stoutly constructed and used as a fender to keep a vessel off a wharf. A buoyant device that is in some places chained to a ship's side to raise her and reduce the draft and allow passage into shallower water.

Cast Off. To let go a line.

Chafing Gear. A winding of canvas, rope, or other matérial around the rigging, spars, and ropes to take the wear.

Chock. An iron casting that serves as a lead for lines to a wharf or other vessels. There are several types—open, closed, and roller chocks.

Cleat. A piece of wood or metal with two horns around which ropes are made fast. *See* Bitts.

Close Aboard. In close proximity to.

Coaming. A raised framework around deck or bulkhead openings and cockpits of open boats to prevent entry of water.

Compass. A direction-indicating instrument. There are two primary types of marine navigational compasses, the *magnetic* and the *gyroscopic*. The *magnetic* compass, which requires no power—being actuated solely by the earth's magnetic field—is usually the more dependable instrument, but it is subject to variation in the earth's magnetic field, acceleration errors, and deviation due to surrounding equipment and other anomalies. Because of this, predetermined corrections must be applied to find true direction. The *gyroscopic* marine compass, on the other hand, is virtually unaffected by outside forces and may be set to always indicate true north (unlike aircraft gyros, which may often require readjustment and are set to indicate *magnetic* north). However, the gyroscopic compass requires a constant and stable source of power for it to operate properly and therefore requires a great deal more effort, time, and equipment to support and maintain it. For this reason, it is unpopular for use in small craft, although a gyro compass will occasionally be found in an officer's motorboat, gig, barge, or large landing craft.

Course Made Good. The course that a vessel actually made good, regardless of the compass course steered, due to adverse currents, wind, etc.

Coxswain. A petty officer in charge of a small boat.

Cross Bearings. Two or more bearings of as many known objects, taken and plotted on the chart. The vessel, being somewhere on each bearing, will be at their intersection. In taking two objects, an error may creep in without detection, but if three objects are used and they plot at or close to the same intersection, the mariner may feel confidence in this position.

Danger Sector. A red sector of a light, indicating the presence of rocks or shoals within it.

Davits. Small cranes that project over the ship's sides for hoisting boats.

Dinghy. A small rowboat. The name is said to come from a Bengal word meaning a small boat belonging to a larger vessel.

Dolphin. A pile or cluster of piles serving as a beacon; a spar mooring buoy; or as a mooring or buffer in the water or on the wharf.

Double-Ended. Having a stern somewhat similar to the bow.

Drag or Drogue. A sea anchor or stopwater. It is either in the form of a spar with a weighted sail attached, or a cornucopia bag. The vessel rides to this device and drifting faster to leeward than the drag, puts a strain on the line, which holds her head to windward. Also called *Sea anchor*.

Even Keel. The trim of a vessel when its keel is parallel with the water surface, or more properly, perhaps, when it takes its designed position for normal trim.

Fairway. A thoroughfare for shipping—midchannel.

Fathom. Six feet. It is the measure of depth in America and many other countries.

Fender. A device to take the shock of contact between ship and wharf or other vessel. There are cork fenders, heavy bags of granulated cork for use at the particular point of collision; fender guards, which are timbers running fore and aft along the side of the vessel; fender spars that float alongside of a wharf to keep a vessel off. There are round logs suspended vertically as fenders. Boat fenders come in many shapes and materials but all are to prevent chafing. Wharves are protected at their corners by clusters of piles, called fender piles.

Fleet Landing. Designated landing area ashore for ships' boats.

Freeboard. Distance from the deck to the waterline.

Gangway. A passageway in the rail of a ship to permit access. An order demanding a passageway among the crew. Often confused with accommodation ladder or gangplank.

Geswarp. A line by which a boat rides at the accommodation ladder. Pronounced "jeswarp."

Gig. A boat assigned to the captain for his personal use.

Grapnel. A small four-pronged anchor, used for dragging for drowned persons, lost articles, or for anchoring small dories or skiffs. Formerly it was employed for holding an enemy ship alongside for hand-to-hand combat.

Gunwale (GUNNEL). The rail of a boat. A gunwale is divided into three parts: *capping* is a flat board on top of the gunwale; *binder* is the part of the gunwale inside of the boat, secured to ribs and capping, bumper is the part of the gunwale on the outside of the boat made of heavy half round often having a metal strap on the outside.

Heave Around. An order to work the capstan. Heave away is

used as an order to pull when the work is heavy, but the term heave around applies to capstan work.

Heave To. To lay a vessel on the wind with helm to leeward, sails shortened down and so trimmed that she will come to and fall off, but always head up out of the trough. A steamer heaving to heads up to the seas, just turning her engines enough to hold her there by using the steerageway. Some steamers are allowed to drift slowly with seas on the quarter using oil, and sometimes long steamers even heave-to in the trough. Hence, to heave-to means to lay a vessel where she takes the seas most comfortably, the thought being to ride out the gale rather than to make progress on the voyage. The less onward motion a vessel has the safer she rides.

Heaving Line. A light line having a manrope knot or small weighted bag at its end to aid in throwing. It is thrown to a pier or another vessel as a messenger for a heavy line.

Helm. The tiller.

Jacob's Ladder. One consisting of served wire rope sides that support rungs usually of iron. Such ladders are found hanging from the stern of a ship, from the boat booms, abaft the masts where trysails and spanker are brailed in, and above the topmast rigging.

Jetty. A breakwater built to protect a river mouth or harbor entrance or to divert or control the current.

Kedge. A light anchor for kedging or warping.

Keel. The backbone of a vessel, from which rise the frames or ribs, stem, and sternpost. The flat keelplate is a plate serving as a keel. A flat-bottomed barge for the conveyance of coal in the British Isles. A barge load of coal is called a keel.

Lee Shore. The coast lying in the direction in which the wind is blowing.

Leeway. The amount a vessel is carried to leeward by force of the wind or current.

Loom of a Light. The loom of a light is its reflection on the clouds when the light itself is below the horizon.

Make For. Head towards.

Monkey Fist. Weighted knot in the end of a heaving line.

Mousing. A piece of small stuff seized across the hook of a block for the purposes of safety.

Oar Lock. A device that has jaws to hold the oar when pulling and a shank that sets in the rail. It is also called row-lock. The distinction sometimes given is: oarlock for steering oar; rowlock for rowing oar. Sometimes a square piece is cut in the gunwale for this purpose, and, again, two pins fitted in sockets serve to hold the oar in rowing. They are called thole pins.

Painter. The rope in the bow of a boat for towing or making fast.

Pelican Hook. A hinged hook that is held in place by a link. When the link is knocked off, the hook collapses. It is also called a slip hook. It is used to make shrouds fast to chain plates and for boat gripes.

Piloting. The navigation of a vessel along shore or into a harbor by means of bearings of landmarks, soundings, and the guidance of buoys and beacons.

Pintle. The hook or pin that fits into the gudgeon and upon which the rudder hangs and turns.

Pooped. A term applied when a wave breaks over the stern.

Preventer. An additional rope or wire placed alongside an overburdened brace or backstay to relieve pressure and prevent an accident.

Rudder Lock. A device at the bottom of a pintle that prevents its rising and unshipping the rudder.

Samson Post. A strong vertical post used for towing and securing.

Scull. To work an oar over the stern at such an angle as to drive a boat ahead. Light oars used in rowing shells, or other boats, are sculls. In fact, with the English especially, to row with two oars is to scull, while rowing is to propel a boat with one man at each oar.

Sea Painter. A long rope not less than 2¾ inch for use in a steamer's boats. It is led forward before lowering the boat and is the last line cast off when launching the boat.

Shove Off. To leave; go away from.

Side Lights. Lanterns or electric lamps located on each side of a vessel, red light to port and green to starboard and so screened as to show from ahead to two points abaft the beam. A screen projects well ahead of the light on the inner side to prevent its being seen across the bow. Also known as running lights.

Skeg. The extreme after part of the keel of a vessel, the portion that supports the rudder post and stern post.

Spar Buoy. A painted spar moored by a mushroom anchor or block of concrete so as to float in an oblique or perpendicular manner.

Splice. To join two ropes by tucking the strands in different ways according to the purpose—short, long, chain, or sail-maker's splice.

Steering Oar. A long oar used as a rudder, especially in whale-boats and lifeboats when the rudder becomes ineffective in a seaway.

Stem. The foremost timber or steel bar in a vessel. It is joined to the keel, and all the planks, or plates, are rabbeted or riveted to it. To stem a current is to proceed and make way against it.

Stern Sheets. The space abaft the thwarts of a small boat.

Strake. A line of planks or plates running the length of a vessel.

Stranded. The condition of a vessel that has run on a strand or, in the U.S., a beach.

Swamped. Overwhelmed by water, or an open boat so filled as to sink or be hopelessly awash.

Thole Pins. Wooden pins that fit in the rail of a boat to hold the oars in place while rowing.

Tide Rips. Patches of broken water caused by rapid tidal currents.

Trail. To let go the oars of a whale boat or gig (single banked) allowing them to swing in the rowlocks until the blades trail aft with the onward motion of the boat. Trailing lines are made fast to the loom of the oars to prevent them from going overboard entirely.

Trice. To haul up.

Tripping Line. A rather general term; it is the line made fast to a sea anchor by which it is hauled aboard.

Turnbuckle. A contrivance made of metal, cylindrical in shape, with an inside thread (one left-handed, the other right-handed) in each end. Into each of these ends screws a threaded eye bolt. A turnbuckle spliced into shrouds, stays, backropes, etc., can be screwed up with great facility and keep a satisfactory tension on the rigging.

Unship. To detach or remove anything from its proper place, as unship a mast, an oar, a capstan bar, etc.

Veer. To pay out anchor chain or rope.

Way. A vessel's movement through the water. Way over the bottom is the actual distance made good in position whether aided or retarded.

Weather Shore. The coast lying in the direction from which the wind is coming.

Whaleboat. A very seaworthy double-ended boat. It is commonly used as a rescue boat and for other utility purposes.

Wherry. A small light rowboat: a small cargo boat of the coast of England that has one large mast stepped well forward and sets a large sail with a gaff but no boom.

Whitecaps. The crested foam seen on the tops of waves in a breeze. The term white horses is often used.

White Water. Breaking wave crests in coastal waters due to oceanic waves shortened and steepened by the shoaling depths.

Wide Berth. A comfortable distance from a ship, a shoal, or the shore.

Windward. The general direction from which the wind blows. It is a point of reference in designating a movement or a location. Also "to weather."

Yaw. To steer badly, as of a ship, usually in running before the wind.

G Aids to Navigation Illustrated

IALA MARITIME BUOYAGE SYSTEM "A"

CARDINAL MARKS

Topmarks are always fitted (when practicable)

Buoy shapes are pillar or spar

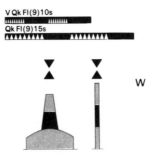

V Qk Fl(9)10s

Qk Fl(9)15s

W

Lights, when fitted, are white, Very Quick Flashing
or Quick Flashing; a South mark also has a Long
Flash immediately following the quick flashes.

Certain FOREIGN WATERS only; does not apply to United States waters

IALA MARITIME BUOYAGE SYSTEM "A"

LATERAL MARKS

PORT HAND   **STARBOARD HAND**

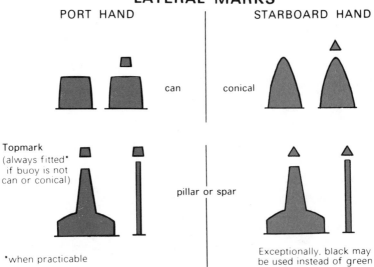

can   conical

Topmark
(always fitted*
if buoy is not
can or conical)

pillar or spar

*when practicable

Exceptionally, black may
be used instead of green

Lights, when fitted, may have any phase characteristic

Examples

    Quick Flashing
Flashing
Long Flashing
Group Flashing

Certain **FOREIGN WATERS** only; does not apply to United States waters

IALA MARITIME BUOYAGE SYSTEM "A"

ISOLATED DANGER MARKS

Topmark
(always fitted)•

Shape: pillar or spar

Light, when fitted, is
white
Group Flashing (2)

Gp Fl(2)

SAFE WATER MARKS

Topmark
(always fitted• if buoy
is not spherical)

Shape: spherical
or
pillar or spar

Light, when fitted, is
white
Isophase or Occulting,
or Long Flashing every
10 seconds

Iso
Occ
L Fl 10s

SPECIAL MARKS

Topmark
(if fitted)

Shape: optional

Light, when fitted, is
yellow
and may have any
phase characteristic not
used for white lights

Examples

Fl Y
Gp Fl (4) Y

Topmark
(if fitted)

If these shapes are
used they will indicate
the side on which the
buoys should be passed

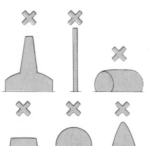

•when practicable

Selected Bibliography

Commercial Books

The Bluejackets' Manual, 20th ed. Annapolis: Naval Institute Press, 1978.

Chapman, Charles F. *Piloting, Seamanship and Small Boat Handling*. New York: The Hearst Corporation, 1968.

Craighead, Frank C., Jr., and Craighead, John J. *How to Survive on Land and Sea*. 4th ed. Annapolis: Naval Institute Press, 1975.

Eastman, Peter F., M.D. *Advanced First Aid Afloat*, 2nd ed. Cornell Maritime Press, Inc., 1974.

Henderson, Richard with Dunbar, Bartlett S. and Brooks, William E. III. *Sale and Power: A Manual of Seamanship*. 3rd ed. Annapolis: Naval Institute Press, 1979.

Hobbs, Richard R. *Marine Navigation I: Piloting*. 2nd ed. Annapolis: Naval Institute Press, 1981.

Hobbs, Richard R. *Marine Navigation II: Celestial and Electronic*. 2nd ed. Annapolis: Naval Institute Press, 1981.

Mack, William P. and Connell, Royal W. *Naval Ceremonies, Customs, and Traditions*. 5th ed. Annapolis: Naval Institute Press, 1980.

Maloney, Elbert S. *Dutton's Navigation and Piloting*. 13th ed. Annapolis: Naval Institute Press, 1978.

Navigation and Operations. Annapolis: Naval Institute Press, 1972.

Nesbitt, Paul H.; Pond, Alonzo W.; and Allen, William H. *The Survival Book*. New York: D. Van Nostrand & Co., Inc., 1959.

Noel, John V., Jr. *Knight's Modern Seamanship*. 15th ed., New York: D. Van Nostrand Co., Inc., 1972.

Robb, Frank. *Handling Small Boats in Heavy Weather*. New York: Quadrangle/The New York Times Book Co., 1965.

Ship Organization and Personnel. Annapolis: Naval Institute Press, 1972.

Shufeldt, H. H., Captain, USNR (Retired). *Using Electronic Calculators to Solve Problems in Navigation*. Annapolis: Naval Institute Press, 1976.

Shufeldt, H. H., Captain, USNR (Retired). *Slide Rule for the Mariner*. Annapolis: Naval Institute Press, 1972.

Tate, William H. *A Mariner's Guide to the Rules of the Road*. Annapolis: Naval Institute Press, 1976.

Tobin, Wallace E., III. *The Mariner's Pocket Companion*. Annapolis: Naval Institute Press, Annual.

Watch Officer's Guide. 11th ed. Annapolis: Naval Institute Press, 1979.

Williams, Jerome; Higginson, John J.; and Rohrbough, John D. *Sea and Air: The Marine Environment*. 2nd ed. Annapolis: Naval Institute Press, 1973.

U.S. Government Publications

Aids to Navigation, CG–193. Department of Transportation, U.S. Coast Guard, July 15, 1977.

American Practical Navigator, HO–9. Defense Mapping Agency Hydrographic/Topographic Center.

Colregs and Demarcation Lines Supplement to Navigation Rules, International-Inland, CG–169–1. July 15, 1977.

International Code of Signals, HO–102, U.S. Naval Oceanographic Office. United States Edition, 1969.

Navigation Rules, International-Inland, CG–169. Department of Transportation, U.S. Coast Guard, May 1, 1977.

U.S. Navy Publications

Boats and Small Craft, NAVSHIPSTECHMAN. Navsea 0901–LP–583–0000.

Boats of the United States Navy, NAVSHIPS 250–452.

Boatswain's Mate 3 & 2, NAVEDTRA 10121–F.

Flags, Pennants & Customs, NWP–13. June, 1977.

Merchant Ship Search and Rescue Manual (MESAR), COMDTINST M16130.1 (OLD CG–421).

National Search and Rescue Manual, NWP–37.

Navy Safety Precautions for Forces Afloat, OPNAVINST 5100.19.

Quartermaster 3 & 2, NAVEDTRA 10149–F.

Search and Rescue Manual, ATP–10B.

Shipboard Helicopter Operating Procedures, NWP–42 (REV.C)

Ships Operations and Regulations Manual, OPNAVINST 3120.32.

Standard First Aid Training Course, Bureau of Naval Personnel, Navy Training Course, NAVPERS 10081.B.

U.S. Navy Regulations, 1973.

Index

150